Table of Contents

Section 1:

Introduction 7

Purpose 8

Organization of This Guide 8

Definition of Terms 8

  Primary Functions of Information 8

    Relational Information 9

    Draft 9

    Document 9

    Publication 9

  Organization of Records 9

    Unitized Records 9

    Transactional Records 9

    Reference 10

Focus on Function, not Form 10

Value of Information 10

  Time Value 10

  Cost of Loss or Delay 11

  Intrinsic Value 11

  Vital 11

  Conclusion 11

Section 2:

Physical Properties and Limitations of Different Media 12

Paper 12

  The Papermaking Process 12

  Recycled Paper 13

  Factors in Deterioration of Paper 14

  Optimal Environmental Conditions for Paper 15

  Properties of Ink 15

  Conclusion 17

Microforms 17

  Physical Description 17

    Film Types 18

    Formats 18

    Film Capacity 19

  Quality of Microforms 20

    Original Quality 20

    Preventing Deterioration 21

    Optimal Conditions for Storage of Film 22

  Microforms: Summed Up 22

Digital Storage 22

  Representation of Information 22

  Compression 23

    Image Compression 23

    Character Compression 24

  Physical Layout of Media 26

    Disks 26

    Tapes 27

  Standards 28

  Conclusion 28

Magnetic Media 28

  Physical Description 28

  Storage and Handling 31

  State of the Art and Advances 31

Optical Media 32

  Physical Description and Recording Methods 32

    CD-ROM Disks 32

    WORM Disks 32

    Magneto-Optical 32

    Phase-Change 32

    Digital Paper 34

  Life Expectancy of Optical Media 35

  Handling Requirements 36

  State of the Art and Advances 36

    Holostore 36

Comparison: Physical Features ·······37

Section 3:

Fundamental Differences in Records ·······41

Inherent Functional Differences ·······41

Underlying Records Structure ·······42

Active Use ·······45

The Birth of a Record ·······45

Distribution and Reproduction·······45

Use and/or Processing ·······45

Review and Approval ·······45

Referrals, Abstractions, and Compilation·······45

Active Storage ·······45

Long Term Storage·······45

Death and Destruction ·······46

Putting It All Together ·······47

Section 4:

Variations and Permutations of Media ·······49

Paper Handling Alternatives ·······49

Micrographics ·······49

Magnetic Media ·······51

Optical Disk ·······52

Publications ·······52

CD-ROM·······52

WORMS and Rewriteable Disks ·······53

Storage of Images ·······53

Media & Disk Access ·······54

Scanning·······55

Transmitting Images ·······55

Displaying and Printing Images ·······55

Processor ·······55

Limitations and Opportunities ·······56

Storage of Machine Readable Data·······56

The Role and Place of Fax Machines
and E-mail ·······56

Section 5:

Finding Records ·······58

Arrangement ·······58

Classification ·······60

Indexes ·······60

Electronic Databases ·······61

Database Output ·······61

Searching Speed ·······61

Flexibility of Searches ·······62

Text Management and Retrieval ·······63

Media Considerations ·······63

Section 6:

Capturing/Converting Information ·······65

Techniques for Capturing and
Exchanging Information ·······65

Data Entry/Exchange·······65

Keystroking ·······65

OCR·······65

Bar Codes ·······67

Voice Input·······68

Data Exchanges·······68

Image Capture ·······70

Filming·······70

Scanning·······70

Conversion ·······71

Converting Existing Collections·······71

When and What To Convert·······71

Estimating Costs and Length of Time·······71

Incorporating Conversions Into
Routine Record Handling·······75

Section 7:

Cost Considerations 76

Direct Costs 76

   Space Costs 76

   Supplies 76

   Labor 76

   Equipment 77

Indirect Costs 77

   Value of Information 77

   Opportunity 77

   Time Compression 77

Conclusion 77

Section 8:

Organizational Considerations 78

Using the Analysis Forms 78

Operational Concerns 78

   Distribution and Movement of Records 84

   Transaction Characteristics 84

   Operating Differences Between Media 87

Records Considerations 87

Organizational Resources 91

   People 91

   Infrastructure 93

   Funding 94

Section 9:

Matching Needs and Media 99

Choosing a Storage Medium for Relational Data 99

Choosing a Storage Medium for Draft Records 99

Choosing a Storage Medium for Documents 99

Choosing a Medium for Publications 114

Acting On Your Decision 114

   Current Medium Is Indicated 114

   A Different Medium Is Indicated 117

Mixing Media 118

Living With Compromises and Making Them Work 118

Section 10:

Approving a Change in Medium 119

Reasons to Change 122

Fits Organization 123

Resource Requirements 123

Solution Selected 124

Potential Problem Areas 124

Media Selection 125

List of Tables

Table 1. Classes of Paper Based on Acid Content 14

Table 2. Common Film Sizes, Usage, Formats and Reduction Ratios......................................19

Table 3. Roll Microfilm Capacity 20

Table 4. Capacity of Common Microfiche Formats 21

Table 5. Storage Required for Bit-Mapped Images (bytes) 23

Table 6. Storage Requirements for Compressed Images in Bytes 25

Table 7. Characteristics of Disk Formatting Schemes 27

Table 8. Primary Characteristics of Magnetic Media 30

Table 9. Optical Formats And Capacities 35

Table 10. Environmental Restrictions for 5.25" WORM Disks ANSI 1987 37

Table 11. Comparison of Media: Physical Characteristics..39

Table 12. Basic Categories of Records 41

Table 13. Primary Records Function and Underlying Structure 43

Table 14. Management Concerns and Needs by Stage of Life and Functional/Structural Combination ..46

Table 15. Variables In Choosing CD-ROM As a Publishing Medium 53

Table 16. Criteria for Choosing Between 12-Inch and 5.25-Inch Optical Disks 54

Table 17. Sample Search Requests....................................62

Table 18. Need to Formalize Methods of Finding Information..64

Table 19. Comparison of Data Entry Methods 69

Table 20. Sustainable Scanning and Filming Rates..........70

Table 21. Personnel Required to Convert 50,000 Documents 74

Table 22. Records Management Job Traits 92

Table 23. Choosing a Medium for Relational Data 100

Table 24. Choosing a Storage Medium for Draft Records..102

Table 25. Choosing a Medium for Publications 115

Table 26. Request Evaluation: Change in Medium........119

Table 27. Comparative Strengths and Weaknesses of Media....................................126

List of Figures and Forms

Figures

Figure 1. Simplified Model of Data Compression Run-Length Encoding Method 24

Figure 2. Disk Formatting Schemes 26

Figure 3. Helical Scan Tape...28

Figure 4. Reading and Writing to an MO Disk 33

Figure 5. Phase Change Reading and Writing 34

Figure 6. Life Cycle of Recorded Information 44

Figure 7. Example of Tri-level Blipping Scheme 51

Figure 8. Hierarchical Arrangement 59

Figure 9. Segment for OCR Identification 65

Figure 10. OCR Matrix with Run Together Letters.........66

Figure 11. Comparison of Data Input Time and Number of Errors When Inputting 50,000 Characters 68

Figure 12. Time Required to Convert 50,000 Documents 73

Figure 13. Using Analysis Forms 78

Forms

Form 1: Operational Concerns...80

Form 2: Records Considerations 89

Form 3: Organizational Resources..................................95

Form 4: Operational Concerns – Documents................104

Form 5: Records Considerations – Documents. 108

Form 6: Organizational Resources – Document 110

Foreword

As technology becomes an integral part of our working lives, we find more and more options regarding the way we handle recorded information. Gone are the days when our only concerns were whether to use manila or kraft file folders in vertical or lateral file cabinets.

With the increase in options, there is a corresponding increase in the number of decisions that must be made. One of the most critical, is the decision regarding the record media.

Optimally, we would like to create records on a medium that will serve our needs for the entire information life cycle. For a variety of reasons, however, this is not always possible. And so, we often find ourselves engaged in unplanned media conversions which frequently prove to be costly, time consuming, and disruptive. It does not have to be that way.

Record systems can be designed that function effectively throughout the entire information life cycle. Necessary media conversions can be planned for as an integral part of the records system operation and can be conducted efficiently and economically. The secret to success in this area–is understanding the media!

This guideline was created by the General Services Administration (GSA) to help Federal agency personnel understand their media options. The following persons are responsible for the Publication:

Ira A. Penn, Management Analyst
Agency Liaison Division

Eugene F. Brown, Management Analyst
Office of Innovative Office Systems

Ann Balough, Consultant
Balough Associates

Questions or comments should be addressed to the General Services Administration, Information Resources Management Service, Agency Liaison Division (KML) Washington, DC 20405.

Section 1: Introduction

Current estimates are that 91% of records are on paper; approximately 4% are on microfilm; magnetic media holds somewhat over 4%; and the rest are on a variety of other media, including compact disc-read only memory (CD-ROM) and optical disks.

Because our choices and uses of media are expanding, we have to define the concept of what a *record* is. It has become a word with many meanings. It is critical for the purposes of this guide to be specific about the meaning of *record*. For this guide, we will use the definitions used by the Federal courts for evidence.

Writings and recordings.
"Writings" and "recordings" consist of letters, words, or numbers, or their equivalent, set down by handwriting, typewriting, printing, photostating, photographing, magnetic impulse, mechanical or electronic recording, or other form of data compilation. (28 USC APP RULE 1001, Rules Of Evidence For U.S. Courts, Article 9.)

Records of regularly conducted activity.
A memorandum, report, record, or data compilation, in any form, of acts, events, conditions, opinions, or diagnoses, made at or near the time by, or from information transmitted by, a person with knowledge, if kept in the course of a regularly conducted business activity, and if it was the regular practice of that business activity to make the memorandum, report, record, or data compilation, all as shown by the testimony of the custodian or other qualified witness, unless the source of information or the method or circumstances of preparation indicate lack of trustworthiness. The term "business" as used in this paragraph includes business, institution, association, profession, occupation, and calling of every kind, whether or not conducted for profit. (28 USC APP RULE 803, Rules Of Evidence For U.S. Courts, Article 8.)

In this context records are information kept (during the regular course of business) to show: something happened, someone did something, particular conditions existed, certain opinions were held, and specific diagnoses made. Both definitions make it clear that this type of information is a *record* regardless of the medium used.

Traditionally, there has been a division between the keepers of data and the keepers of records. In legal terms, this has always been an arbitrary and artificial division. In practical terms it came about because the functions of the two groups had little in common: computers required specialized knowledge, were centralized, and held very little information needed as evidentiary documentation. The keepers of data kept very small amounts of information under very tight controls. The keepers of records dealt with massive amounts of information under rather loose control. This has changed. The personal computer (PC) has brought computing to the masses. Mainframes and software packages have improved. Computer storage is not as expensive. Word processing is de facto in almost all offices. So more important information that falls into the area of evidentiary documentation is being kept on media other than paper. Since the masses are creating and controlling more of this information, there are fewer controls. The length of time that we depend on computerized information is also increasing.

Organizations are contending with the prospect of more records, created in more ways, stored on more media, and in the hands of more people. This causes problems in controlling the information and having the right information, where and when it is needed. The need for better systems of managing records has also grown. Fortunately, technology offers better tools for managing records, in addition to the media options. Often the decision to change to a new medium is an effort to gain more control of and access to records.

The possibilities have become staggering, and at times rather confusing. The plethora of alternatives makes the task of choosing an appropriate medium for records even more difficult. Adding to the complexity is the capability for information to reside on several media during its lifetime. The problem is often not to choose the perfect medium for a set of records, but to choose the best mix of media at various times during the life cycle of the information. For example, census information may start life as a handwritten form. At this point in time aggregate information, rather than individual information is needed. So, the information is input and stored as electronic data. The electronic data can then be compiled and published, possibly as a CD-ROM. This makes the census information available to large numbers of people. When the information on individuals passes into the public domain and gains genealogical and historical value, interest in the individual data is renewed. The original forms may then be microfilmed and widely distributed. Thus the same information may be stored on a variety of media to serve a variety of purposes.

Determining the best medium, or media mix, is not a simple task. There is rarely one correct decision, but many poor ones. The ability to automate records comes at a high price, not only in equipment, but in organizational resources. There are many variables. Most important are to know your organization, the functions the records serve, and how technology can be used to meet your specific needs.

Purpose

This publication is designed to help Federal Government managers choose the mix of media for records that will best suit the needs of both the organization and the nature of the information. There are no easy answers. Just as there are no generic organizations, there are no "one-size fits all" solutions. This publication will give you more information about the available alternatives, a framework for analyzing your needs, and an approach for matching your needs with a suitable technology. You provide the common sense and knowledge of your organization.

Organization of This Guide

This guide will be more useful if the entire contents are at least scanned initially. The topics build on each other:

- First, the physical properties of available storage media are discussed in Section two. When evaluating media and technology, focus on real differences rather than differences of habit. It is important to differentiate between what is not possible and what has not been done.

- The next part of the discussion is concerned with some of the fundamental differences in records. If these differences are not taken into consideration when planning a records management system, the system may have flaws that no change in technology or medium can compensate for.

- Section four discusses some of the different ways each medium is implemented in records management and how the implementation may affect the management of information. There are basic operational differences between microfilm and microfiche, for example, even though the same medium is utilized.

- Ways of finding information are discussed next. Identification and retrieval are an integral part of any records management system. This is also an area where technological advances can have a tremendous impact, regardless of the technology.

- Information exists first in our minds, then we inscribe it. After putting the information on one medium, it may be converted to another. In order to manage information well, we need to understand how the inscription and conversion process affects the management of information. The capturing and conversion of information is discussed in Section seven.

- Section seven examines how differences between media impact on costs for technology, conversions, and personnel.

- Following that is a discussion of organizational considerations. Without a good understanding of how the information is used by an organization, it is impossible to make a good choice of media or technology.

- Section nine draws on the information in all the previous sections and provides a framework for matching needs and media.

- The last section is a guide for managers who approve changes in media: what types of questions to ask, what to look for, and how to evaluate a request.

Definition of Terms

The choice of medium needs to be closely linked with the function and purpose of the records stored. It must also take into consideration how the need for the information changes over time.

This section is not really so much a dictionary definition of terms as it is an explanation and clarification of the roles of information. It is important to read this section, not necessarily for the virtue and clarity of the definitions, but for the conceptual basis it provides for the rest of the discussion.

The terms defined are arranged into two different groups: the first is the primary function of the information and the second is the basic organization of the information.

Primary Functions of Information

We keep records for many reasons, the worst of which is habit—keeping records because they have always been kept. To do a good job of applying technology to records, we must understand the records.

Relational Information

Relational information is commonly referred to as data dis-crete pieces of information that are linked together to form a record. This type of information is most commonly found in electronic databases. Individual pieces of information are manipulated and linked to show logical or natural associations between and among them. Paramount concerns for data are accuracy, speed of access, and the ability to pull the right pieces of information together when confronting a need. The primary function of relational information is to provide current information quickly.

Draft

The primary function of draft information is to provide working copies. It is information that is being worked on — manuscripts, letters, contracts, etc. The information is still subject to change and revision. Once a draft is signed and dated — authenticated — it becomes a document. A common source of draft information is word processors. The use of magnetic media for storing draft information has made it important. Until recently, draft copies had little value and were usually discarded after the final copy was produced. Now, because draft information that is stored electronically can be reused and manipulated to create new documents it can have significant value. Technology has given a new function to draft data: a time-savings when producing future documents.

Document

A document differs from the other types of information. Its function is to record and prove that an action has been taken or a decision made. *It is authenticated and should not be altered.* After signing and sealing, no changes should be made. Ninety percent of information stored in offices falls into this category. Choosing a medium for documents is very complex and depends to a large extent upon the purposes the document serves. This is the type of record that most often serves as evidentiary documentation. Safe-guarding the original content and basic form of this type of document is important if it is ever to be used in court.

Publication

Some information is needed by so many people that it is published. In this guide, we will refer to publications as copies of those writings specifically intended for an audience outside the department of origin. Published writings may be one-time or periodic. They include such things as catalogs, reference materials, and regulations. While the original of the publication is a document, the copies serve a different function. Important considerations in choosing a medium for publication are the expenses of publishing and distribution.

Organization of Records

The juxtaposition of time and function of the record impose some basic requirements for how the records must be organized.

Unitized Records

Some types of information have to be accessed as a group. Examples of unitized records are personnel files, project designs, loan records, contract files, etc. The records may be collected over a period of years. In order to make good decisions, access to all the information is needed, not just the most recent. For example, a decision about a long-term project may require reviewing documents that date back five years. These records form a history and should be used as a unit. The records are not kept for a fixed period of time. The information is kept primarily to record specific actions and decisions and to provide a basis for future decisions. The length of time the records are useful depends on the occurrence of some event: an employee retires, a contract is terminated, a project is replaced. Until the event occurs, all the information in the unit needs to be kept. The organization of these records should be such that the user knows of the existence of all information in the unit.

Transactional Records

Transactional records substantiate the occurrence of an event at a specific point in time. These records may be grouped by any number of criteria, but the time of creation is the dominant factor in how the records are organized. The records from a given time period are kept together and treated in a similar manner. As time passes, their value declines. For example, accounts payable records are kept together by fiscal year. The organization may keep two years of files on hand and store older files. After a given period all of them are destroyed because at a certain point there are no longer any actions that would be based on that information. The primary differentiation between unitized records and transactional records is the ability to predict how long a record is to be kept. It is easy to determine the life of an accounts payable check; the length of time a contract amendment will be kept cannot be predicted with any certainty.

Reference

Unlike the other two classes of records, transactional and unitized, reference information is not kept to record actions, only to provide information upon which to base decisions. The time this information is needed varies greatly. A supply clerk may receive a new supply catalog every month. The old one has no value and can be discarded. The same supply clerk may also have a copy of a procurement regulation that is three years old. Until that regulation is replaced, it is necessary to maintain it. There is no predictable pattern to the length of time reference material needs to be kept. It varies with the function and how fast it is replaced. These records should not be organized by date. When it is, pertinent information is often buried in inactive files. Unitized records can be organized by the case, person, contract, etc. that they refer to. Transactional data is organized by date and type. However, the need for reference information is more difficult to predict. Therefore, reference data is often the most challenging to organize.

Focus On Function, Not Form

The beauty and elegance of a piece of technology may lure buyers to find a way to use it — a solution in search of a problem. This misplaced focus is responsible for the failure or poor performance of many systems. When choosing a technology for recordkeeping, focus on the function of the record. We keep records for the information they contain. The media has absolutely no impact on the information contained in a record. Changing media influences accessibility, usability, safety, integrity, and the storage costs of information. It does not change the content.

Changing media is analogous to changing location. When you get a memo from the boss, you have a variety of options. You may throw it onto your desk, stick it in a drawer, tack in on a bulletin board, or file it away neatly. Finding the memo is quicker and easier when it is on the bulletin board than when it is stuffed in the desk drawer. On your desk it is readily at hand (maybe), but subject to coffee stains and donut crumbs or being shuffled in with the

wrong set of papers. Regardless of where you keep the information, the content is not affected. The memo says the same thing. It may be harder to find, get lost, be misplaced, or in more danger because of the location, but the information is constant. A change in media is very much like a change in location. It does not change the information, but it does change our ability to use it.

It is not possible to choose a good technology for records without understanding the role played by the records and their value to the organization.

Value of Information

Management teachings traditionally focus on scarce resources — money, people, space, time, etc. Information, and the records upon which it is stored, is a perverse asset. We have far *too much* of it. Important information is often buried in dross. Records make no *direct* contribution to productivity. Compounding the problem, record value changes with time and circumstance. Records management, unlike personnel management, accounting, computer science, and finance, is not taught as a routine part of business curriculums. Too often records are looked upon as a cost rather than a resource. If information is managed only to minimize costs, the organization and those it serves will suffer.

Because we are not usually taught how to deal with information as resource, it is doubly important that we pay careful attention to how it is managed, and do not make the mistake of managing it in the same way we manage scarce resources. With an overabundance of a commodity, we have to discriminate. The value of all information is not equal and it changes over time.

Time Value

The number of referrals to records decreases as the records age. Eighty-five percent of filed records are never referenced and 95% of those references are to records that are less than three years old. Transactional records, especially, lose importance very quickly as they age. The value of this type of information is primarily operational — it is needed to make good decisions or to initiate timely actions. Knowing where these records are and getting to them quickly is important for a relatively short time. Then the information is replaced by more current information or it just "wears out" because it

is no longer true or important. Unitized records and reference information may not wear out as quickly, but the value
does diminish with time.

Cost of Loss or Delay

The value of information is enhanced by having it when and
where it is needed. Finding a cancelled check three years
after a payment dispute is ineffectual. Delays in finding
information can mean some tasks are suspended, deadlines
are not met, and that extra work is required to find information and get it to the people who need it. For example, if
routine phone requests for information can be handled on
the spot, time is saved returning phone calls. Only the organization can determine what are acceptable delays.

Acceptable speed of access is a function of the price paid for
increased access versus the losses incurred by delays. The
price of losing information varies with the situation and the
information. Some information is unique and cannot be
replaced. Other information can be reconstructed, so a loss
may mean the cost of reconstructing information. Another
cost of delay and loss is the impact of decisions made with
poor or incomplete information. For example, a contract
may improperly be renewed because the complaints received
about the contractor's performance have been misplaced and
were not available when the decision to renew was made.

Intrinsic Value

A few documents have inherent value. The Constitution is
one such document. The intrinsic value is usually historic
and/or esthetic. For these documents the medium is generally an integral part of the value and the emphasis may need
to be placed on preserving the original. As a part of this,
copies may be made on a more durable medium for daily
use and the original preserved in its original form.

Vital

Vital records are those which cannot be replaced immediately after a disaster strikes and are essential to the continued
existence of an organization. Only four to six percent of
records fall into this class. However, it they are destroyed,
the organization may suffer irreversible damage. Private
organizations may even pass out of existence. Government
entities will survive a loss of a vital records, but their ability
to function can be severely impaired. For example, the loss
of tax records can be very detrimental, seriously reducing the
amount of tax collected. Because vital records are so essential, safety of the records is paramount.

Conclusion

All information in an organization is not equal. The same
information is not equally important at all times in its life
cycle. For most organizations a single medium is unlikely to
serve all needs. In fact, as more media become available the
right mix continues to change. The importance of understanding the organization, its information needs, and managing information resources increase in importance. Good
management will always be more important than the medium itself.

Factors In Deterioration of Paper

Acid, light, heat, humidity, air pollutants, dust, fungus, insects, vermin, and hard or prolonged usage all cause deterioration in paper.

Acidity is the primary cause of deterioration in paper. High acidity causes cellulose fibers to break down. Since the bonds between the fibers is what holds paper together, eventually the paper flakes and crumbles.

Most papers used today are produced from pulp processed by acid cooking. The American Society for Testing and Materials (ASTM) has classified four types of paper based on its pH content (a lower pH means higher acidity).

damage in paper by changing its dimensions, increasing physical stress, promoting the effect of water as a chemical agent, and encouraging the growth of fungi. In high humidity paper absorbs additional water and changes shape — it warps, wrinkles, and tears. Then, when the humidity decreases, moisture is released. The physical stresses of the dimensional changes causes the fibers to break apart. Dyes and inks tend to fade in higher humidity. Water also acts as a chemical agent. It is an important agent in acid hydrolysis. It not only works with acid in the paper, but helps to bring acid to the paper from other sources: folders, rubber bands, pollution, etc.

Table 1: Classes of Paper Based on Acid Content

Type	Acidity	Life Expectancy
One	pH 7.5-9.5	Several hundred years
Two	pH 6.5-7.5	50-100 years
Three	pH 5.5-6.5	About 50 years
Four	pH under 5.5	Under 50 years

Light causes chemical reactions in paper that lead to discoloration and embrittlement. Lignin reacts with light and turns yellow. The shorter the wavelength of the light, the greater the damage. Daylight is the most damaging and incandescent is the least.

High heat makes paper dry and brittle. Constant and rapid changes in temperature are even more damaging because paper is made of component materials that absorb heat and expand at different rates. The changes in the dimensions cause fibers to expand and contract, tearing apart the bonds, and leading to structural breakdown. The rate of chemical reactions in cellulose doubles for every 9°F increase in temperature. As a result of the chemical reaction the fibers shorten, breaking the bonds that hold the paper together.

Paper is hygroscopic (absorbs water easily). Humidity causes

Air pollutants such as sulfur dioxide, hydrogen sulfide, nitrogen oxide, and ozone contribute to the deterioration of paper. Some combine with the water in the atmosphere to form acids. Ozone causes embrittlement. Dust and dirt particles in the air also damage paper. They absorb and carry pollutants. They begrime and abrade paper and, because the particles are hygroscopic, facilitate the action of water.

Because cellulose is an excellent food source, it attracts living organisms. Fungi including molds and mildew grow on paper. Given the right temperature and humidity, they flourish. Both paper and ink are attacked. The spores are very resilient and long-lived. After proper environmental conditions are restored, spores become dormant, await a suitable environment, and grow again — even after ten to fifteen years. Over seventy varieties of insects, including bookworms (actually the larvae of several species of beetle), cockroaches, silverfish, and termites, find paper a tasty treat. Both the feasting and the dirt tracked in by the insects contribute to deterioration of paper. Vermin, particularly mice and rats, not only eat paper, but also carry in insects and dirt.

The other enemy of paper is people. Fortunately most don't eat it, but careless and excessive handling — tears, wrinkles, abrasion, spills, stains, holes from binding and stapling, etc. — speed the deterioration process.

Optimal Environmental Conditions for Paper

Temperatures between 65°F and 72°F are best for storing paper. For every 9°F the temperature is lowered the life of the paper nearly doubles, because the chemical activity slows to half the previous rate. At 100° to 150°, deterioration is very rapid — paper can break down completely in as little as eighteen years. Even more devastating than continual high temperature are fluctuations in temperature. This leads to deterioration from both fiber breakage and water damage. Temperature should not vary more than 2.5°F.

The humidity should be maintained at 45-55% relative humidity. This will prevent both desiccation and fungus. Sharp fluctuations are extremely destructive.

Since acidity is a major cause of deterioration, it would seem that acid-free paper should last longer than other papers. This can be true, but the supplies of acid-free paper are limited and more expensive. Acid-free pinfeed computer paper costs at least twice as much as conventional pin-feed paper. Until the 1960's, the technology to produce acid-free paper on a large scale was not available. Converting from acid to alkaline processes is time consuming and slow. However, the concerns of both the publishing industry and environmentalists about the quality of paper and damage caused from acidic by-products of paper production have combined to increase the number of manufacturers producing acid-free paper. Nevertheless, most of the paper available today still has a pH between 4.5 and 5.5, with a life expectancy of under fifty years.

Even with acid free paper, acid damage is possible. Acid is insidious. Acid will migrate from page to page. Acid-free paper cannot be stored with acidic paper, bound with acidic bindings (rubber bands are extremely acidic), placed in acidic folders, or stored in an acidic box. Only acid free paper stored in acid free containers that are exposed only to other acid free papers, will last as long as expected. Even then, atmosphere can cause some acid damage.

Permanent paper must meet the following standards: an alkaline pH (7.5 -8.5), folding endurance, tear-resistance, and an alkaline reserve (2-3%) — to resist acidic elements in the environment. With proper handling, permanent paper can be expected to last several centuries.

Properties of Ink

Paper alone does not constitute a document. Information has to be fixed upon it in some manner. The clarity, contrast, and permanence of the inscription is important to the overall quality of the document. While a fair amount of attention is paid to paper, very little attention is focused on how the image upon it is achieved.

Ink is a primary source of inscription. Toners, however especially those used in printers and copiers are fast becoming as prevalent — particularly in the office. Special papers that aid in creating images are also growing in importance and quantity. Inks and toners need to adhere to the paper and provide images that last: the print should not fade or rub off.

Ink has four components: colorants, dyes or pigments that provide the color; a vehicle, which carries the colorants and upon drying, binds it to the paper; additives which influence printability especially drying speed and film characteristics (how thin and evenly it spreads); and solvents which reduce ink viscosity and adjust drying ease.

There are two varieties of ink — printing and writing. Printing ink is basically a specialized paint. Writing ink is a dye. The pigment (printing) or the dye (writing) is contained in a carrier yielding a fluid, paste, or powder that is applied to and dried onto paper.

Relatively few documents that concern records managers are published by printing presses. More important are the inks used in typewriter and printer ribbons, in ink-jet printers, and in pens.

Several types of ribbons are available. Fabric ribbons have a woven base, often of nylon. The vehicle must be able to draw the ink to the paper where it can penetrate quickly, but without excessive wicking. Very strong pigmentation is required because there is a low ratio of pigment to vehicle. Film ribbons are solid ink applied to a polymer base.

Typewriters and printers using a print element, a daisy-wheel, dot-matrix pins, or belts (such as in many line printers) transfer ink by pressing the ribbon to the paper in a pattern that corresponds to the character being formed. Thermal printers use heat (and sometimes pressure) to melt ink from the ribbon and transfer it to the paper. Ink from a film ribbon has a much waxier base. Because the pigment to vehicle ratio is higher, the image tends to be darker. Unless heat is applied along with pressure, the images from film ribbons generally do not penetrate the paper to the same extent as the ink from film ribbons. This lack of penetration limits wicking, making the image crisper, but the ink may not adhere well to the paper fibers.

Ink jet printers spray ink onto the page. An electrostatic charge attracts the ink drops and forms letters. Surface tension, viscosity and conductivity are very important in formulating the ink. Earlier ink jet printers used liquid ink, but this caused clogging problems and limited the popularity of the printers. Solid inks that are melted as needed have eliminated these problems and are contributing to the growing demand for ink jet printers. Ink jet printers often require papers that are less permeable, in order to control wicking.

Writing inks are solutions colored by soluble dyes. They dry by evaporation of the solvent. The early writing inks were made of carbon dispersed in water or oil. Later, metallic salts and tannic acid were used. Tannic acid reacts with the salts and colors the ink either black or brown. Salts were replaced with indigo, first, and then synthetic dyes. Fountain pen inks are still made in basically the same way. Modern blue-black ink is colored blue by dye. When exposed to oxygen, the blue fades and the metal tannate oxidizes to a black color. This ink is permanent and will not fade from the paper. Felt-tip pens are formed by textile fibers bound together with a resin, leaving enough air spaces to allow capillary action. Thus, the ink flows through the fibers to the paper. The ink is similar to ordinary ink except it has a higher moisture content to prevent the tip from clogging. Some plotters and printers use specially-designed felt tip pens. Due to the high moisture content, felt pens tend to wick on some papers. Ballpoint pens transfer ink to paper from the surface of a ball that is .7 to 1.0 millimeters in diameter. The volume of ink delivered is very small. The ink contained in a small ballpoint refill will draw a continuous line 1500 to 2000 yards long. The same amount of fountain pen ink will draw a line only 80 to 100 yards long. Because the quantity of ink transferred is small, the coloring must be very intense. To prevent clogging, the inks are carefully filtered and contain very slow-drying solvents. Because the component dimensions for pen design vary from one pen to another, ballpoint inks are designed to match the pen. Ballpoint inks dry quickly and do not tend to wick much.

Toners and electrostatic reproduction technology are used in most copy machines, laser printers, and some fax machines. Toner is composed of finely ground carbon particles suspended or combined with a resin. It may be powdered or dry. The carbon provides the color and the resin bonds the carbon to the paper. Toner formulas, particularly the resin base, are becoming increasingly complex. In indirect electrostatic (xerographic) printing, an image is formed on an intermediate surface, usually a drum or belt. The image attracts charged toner particles which are transferred to an oppositely charged piece of paper. Heat or pressure is used to fuse the toner. The direct electrostatic process utilizes coated papers that are photoreceptive. The image is created directly on the paper. The toner is attracted directly to the paper and then fused. All toners are specifically formulated for each machine. The resin formula determines the heat and pressure combination used to fuse toner to the paper.

Specially coated papers can be used to replace the need for ink or toner. One process uses heat to change the color of the paper surface with a heated printing element. This method is very quick and quiet. Another method is to coat paper with microcapsules. This is the method used for "carbonless" papers used in multi-part forms. The dye capsules are burst by pressure from a pen, printer, or typewriter. Acids in the coating of the paper react with the dye and fix it.

Archivists and paper companies have done a fair amount of research on the properties of paper. Paper can be artificially aged by using high temperatures. In this way the impact of different components on the life of paper can be accurately assessed. However, the same type of testing does not work with ink and toner. The deterioration of ink and toner is much harder to research. High heat changes the bond between the vehicle and the paper, but the changes are not the same as in naturally aged papers and inks. In addition to the lack of an artificial aging process, most formulas for inks and toners are proprietary. Formulations change rapidly, and with the increasing pace of printer and copier development the rate of change is increasing. Many of the inks and toners in use today are new formulations. Little is known about how age and storage conditions affect inks and toners —

particularly their adhesion to paper and proneness to fading.

In writing instruments, there does seem to be a correlation between ink price and permanence. Water-based inks are not as durable. Color pigments, and therefore colored inks, fade faster and may not reproduce as well. Inks described as permanent usually are. Even if the ink fades, the impression from a fountain pen or ballpoint lasts. Ballpoint pens with dark blue or black ink are generally best for important documents. Felt tip pens leave no impression and the inks are water soluble, so they should be avoided when a fairly permanent impression is needed.

Most printer ribbons and toner formulas are too new to have stood the test of time. However, there are a few guidelines that may help prolong the life of the image.

- Try to achieve maximum contrast at the time of creation. Replace ribbons regularly. Use only toners designed for a particular machine.

- Follow paper recommendations. Some machines need smooth papers to ensure good adhesion by inks or toners. Others require special coatings that limit ink penetration and wicking. Others are better if no coating is used. Coated papers may damage some machines.

- Stacking should be limited. Toners and inks applied with heat are thermoplastic. With heat or pressure, they may migrate from the original. For the same reasons, they should also be kept away from vinyl surfaces. Sometimes the image moves from the top of the page to the bottom of the surface above it, especially to vinyl.

- Avoid colored inks and toners. Black pigments and dyes tend to be the most stable. Colored pigments are less stable and more subject to fading.

- Use specially coated papers (used for thermal printers and some fax machines) and microencapsulation papers only for short-term documents as these images are very sensitive to pressure, heat, and light.

- Keep machines well maintained.

- Minimize handling to reduce the amount of abrasion.

- Keep the exposure to light to a minimum, especially sunlight. This helps to minimize fading.

Conclusion

Partially because paper is so familiar, we rarely think about it. Paper is the de facto standard for media and we tend to think of it as permanent. Understanding that paper is a mass of cellulose fibers and chemical additives gives us a truer picture of a medium that is chemically active and subject to constant change. All paper is not created equal, so the lifetime of all paper is not equal. Nor can we ignore the inks and toners used. Perfectly preserved paper is of little value if the printing has rubbed off or faded.

Microforms

In 1925 a bank clerk, G. L. McCarthy, filed a patent for equipment to film bank checks. In 1928 Eastman Kodak Company produced the first commercial 16mm microfilmer. Since then the use of microforms has grown to about four percent of all business records. A distant second to paper, it still represents a lot of images. More than seventy percent of businesses with 1,000 plus employees use some form of microform. One-third of computer output is printed onto microfilm. So while the percentage of records on film is small, the impact of microform upon records management is important.

Physical Description

Photography and the production of microforms are essentially the same technology. Microforms are photographic images that are 20 to 150 times smaller than the original. Smaller images are possible, but not very readable. Specialized films, cameras, and processing have been developed because microforms involve photographing flat black-and-white images instead of three-dimensional objects. Color microfilm is available, but not widely used. It is not discussed in this guide. Advances in film and lens technology often carry over into the microfilm area.

All microforms are small images on film. The differences are the type of film used, the format, the size of the film, and image reduction.

Film Types

Three basic types of film are used in microfilming: silver halide, diazo, and vesicular. There are also some unconventional films used in limited applications. The procedures for processing films are directly related to their physical properties.

Silver halide is the film most commonly used to produce master film. It is also the process that most closely resembles conventional black-and-white photography. The film is a gelatin emulsion containing fine grains of metallic silver coated on one side of a film base — either cellulose acetate or polyester. The image that is created when light is reflected from the surface of the document through the camera lens to the film is held in the emulsion. The image on the emulsion is a latent image. It is best to develop the film as soon as possible, because latent images fade as the time between exposure and development lengthens. Developing is done in total darkness and to exacting standards. The image is fixed in a series of chemical baths. The portion of the emulsion struck by the light hardens and remains fixed to the base of the film. After fixing, the film is washed to remove residual chemicals — especially sodium thiosulfate which acts as a fixing agent. Silver film has a negative mode: it reverses the original. Non-reversal silver halide film is available, but not common. So, original silver film produces a negative image — white on black. Prints (or copies) made on silver film are positive.

Diazo film is used primarily for making duplicates and for intermediate masters made directly from the original silver halide film. Diazo film has either a cellulose acetate or polyester base coated with a resin containing diazonium salts. Diazo is used for making direct contact prints. Because there is only a 4% loss in definition for each generation of diazo, it is a popular film for duplicates. Duplicates are made by placing the diazo film in direct contact with the original and transmitting UV light through the transparent image to expose the diazo film. The light decomposes the diazo component so that it cannot turn dark in the presence of ammonia. Anhydrous or hydrous ammonia is used depending upon the film and processor. Dry diazo film has the chemicals needed for developing incorporated in the resin. Heat develops the film. This makes office duplicators possible without the safety hazards and expense of venting for ammonia. Diazo film does not change the mode of the film it copies from. If the original is negative, so is the copy. Positive copies are made from positive originals.

Vesicular film is an emulsion of stable diazonium salts dispersed in a polymer layer. As in diazo film, the diazonium layer decomposes when exposed to UV light. As it decomposes, nitrogen gas is given off and confined in the polymer layer. The film is then re-exposed to high intensity UV light. This causes the gas to expand in the softened polymer and form tiny bubbles or vesicles, fixing the image. Since no wet or chemical processing is involved, vesicular film is inexpensive to produce. It is used mainly for Computer Output Microfilm (COM) and to make copies. Vesicular is a reversal film. It produces positives from negative originals and vice versa. Non-reversal vesicular film is available, but not common.

Silver halide, diazo, and vesicular film are by far the most widely used films, but there are two types of unconventional films that are found in a number of applications: dry silver and updateable. Dry silver has the chemicals needed for developing embedded in the film. Heat activates the developing process; no wet processing is required. Because all of the films mentioned to this point have one thing in common (images cannot be added after exposure), special updateable films have been developed. They are used in special cameras that allow the addition of images. There are two varieties: electrostatic and photoplastic. Electrostatic film has a photoconductive layer coated on a polyester base. The film is sensitized by an electrostatic charge and an image is created with toner. With photoplastic film the images are formed by a pattern of electrostatic charges. Then the image is fixed by heating and deforming the film then cooling it into the new shape, complete with images. With photoplastic film, images can be erased and replaced.

Formats

The basic microform formats are roll film, microfilm jackets, microfiche, card jackets, and aperture cards. Film most commonly comes in 16, 35, and 105 millimeter (mm) widths. Some applications use 8mm or 70mm widths, but these are rare. Film varies in thickness from 2.5 to 7 mils thick. The most common thickness is 5 mils but 2.5 mils is becoming more popular because of the higher density. Standard reels for processed microfilm hold 100 feet of 5 mil film or 215 feet of 2.5 mil film. Most new automated microfilm readers accept both 5 mil and 2.5 mil film.

Roll microfilm is a continuous strip of images. Microfiche are card-size strips of film with images laid in a grid. Ultrafiche are microfiche that have a very high reduction

Table 2: Common Film Sizes, Usage, Formats, and Reduction Ratios

Film Width	Uses	Formats	Reduction Ratios[1]
16mm	Small documents	Roll Film Jackets	24x 27x 29x 30x 40x
35mm	Newspapers	Aperture Cards Roll Film Jackets	16x 24x 30x
105mm	Microfiche of business documents. Computer-output micrfiche and film. Micropublishing. Very large engineering drawings and maps. Documents that cannot have a high reduction ratio.	Microfilm, Ultrafiche Roll Film	24x 42x 48x 150x

[1]An infinite number of reduction ratios are possible, these are the ones most commonly used.

ratio (150x or more). Microfilm jackets are two pieces of thin polyester sealed together on two sides and divided into channels for either 16 or 35 mm film. Strips of film are inserted into the channels. Copies of film jackets are often made onto microfiche. Card jackets are similar, but use a cardboard jacket that often has other information written on it. Aperture cards are cards with room for a single image — usually 35mm but occasionally 16mm. Section 4 discusses microform formats and related equipment in more detail.

Microform images are reduced copies of the original. A reduction of 24x means that the image is 1/24th the size of the original. The amount of reduction is determined by the lens of the camera and the focal length. Practice has established standard reductions ratios for each film format. Table 2 shows the most common film widths, the types of documents most commonly filmed on that size, and the formats and reduction ratios used.

Extremely high reduction ratios are feasible, but the resolution of the copy may suffer. Low resolution makes the images difficult to read. The standard reduction ratios have come about, in part, because they offer satisfactory resolutions.

Film Capacity

Capacity of each film format varies with the size of the film, the size of the original, and the reduction ratio. The formula to determine capacity is:

$$\frac{\text{Reduction ratio x Length of film (in inches)}}{\text{Feed length of paper in inches + 1 inch}} = \text{Images/roll}$$

The feed length is the length of the side of paper fed into the camera. It generally corresponds to the paper width.

Table 3: Roll Microfilm Capacity

	Reduction Ratios							
	100 Foot Roll Film[1]				215 Foot Roll Film[1]			
Feed Length[2]	16x	24x	30x	48x	16x	24x	30x	48x
5 inches	3040	4560	5700	9120	6720	10080	12600	20160
8.5 inches	1920	2880	3600	5760	4244	6366	7958	12733
11 inches	1520	2280	2850	4560	3360	5040	6300	10080
14 inches	1216	1824	2280	3648	2688	4032	5040	8064

[1]*A five foot allowance is given for leaders, flashes, etc.*

[2]*Usually the width of the document.*

Roll microfilm capacity has to allow for a leader and some space for documents called flashes that identify the roll and breaks between groups of documents. Table 3 shows the number of images for 100 and 215 feet at certain standard reduction ratios.

Standard microfiche is a piece of film 105mm by 148mm (4" x 6") that has documents arranged in columns and rows and a top strip containing eye-readable title information. Table 4 shows the capacities for common microfiche formats. Ultrafiche is usually 150X and carries 3,280 letter-size images. Parts and maintenance manuals, book collections, and some periodicals are published on ultrafiche.

Aperture cards were designed to permit fast filing and retrieval of large engineering drawings and maps and to produce reduced size hardcopy through various photographic or "blueprint" processes. They consist of an opening (aperture) set in a card. The card is usually an EAM (Electronic Accounting Machine) card (also referred to as a punch card). The film is held by pressure-sensitive adhesive or inserted into a transparent sleeve. Access data may be keyed on the card, along with the eye-readable interpretation. Usually the aperture holds a single frame of 35 mm film.

Quality of Microform
Original Quality

An important definition of film quality is the resolution or sharpness of the image. Resolution is a measure of the sharpness of the lines of the image on film. At lower resolutions, the patterns of letters blend and blur. Documents cannot be read. The standard test to measure resolution is to film a resolution test chart and examine the film image with a microscope. The chart has identical patterns of decreasing size. Each is given a numerical value. The test is a subjective measure of how clearly patterns can be recognized after filming. Resolution is generally stated in terms of lines per millimeter with higher numbers indicating higher resolution. The generally used standard is 120 lines per millimeter (or 120 LPM). Higher resolutions are needed at higher reduction

Table 4: Capacity of Common Microfiche Formats

Document Size	Reduction Ratio	Number of Columns	Number of Rows	Number of Frames	Use
Letter	24X	14	7	98	Documents or COM
Legal	24X	9	7	63	Documents or COM
Letter	42X	25	13	325	COM
Legal	42X	16	13	208	COM
Letter	48X	28	15	420	COM
Legal	48X	18	15	270	COM

ratios and when the individual character recognition is very important such as lists of numbers, pricing, or engineering documentation. Resolution degrades with each generation of copy, so high resolution in the original is essential. Resolution is a function of both the camera lens and the film. Good resolution comes from good lenses and good film. Poor resolution can also be an indication of poor camera operating procedures.

Another measure of quality is contrast, the difference between the light and dark areas of the image. It is measured by a densitometer. The numerical standard for good film is between 1.0 and 1.2. If the density reading is lower, the film is underexposed. If it is higher, the film is overexposed. In both situations the contrast is poor, making it harder to read copies.

Resolution and contrast must be built into the film from the beginning and then protected. Film stock should not be stored for long periods of time before use and should be processed as soon after exposure as possible. In order for microforms to maintain quality, both the emulsion contain-

ing the image and the base to which it is attached must be protected. If you intend to keep film in good shape for a long time, the original copy cannot be used for anything except to make masters for copying.

Preventing Deterioration

Light, especially ultraviolet light, discolors images and increases the brittleness of the film base. Silver and vesicular film are more resistant to light but diazo film images can fade rapidly.

Most films have a plastic base and will degrade to some degree over time. High temperature can greatly accelerate the process. Short-term exposure to high temperatures does not drastically affect silver or diazo film, but vesicular film will undergo a complete image loss above 175°F. The emulsion softens and the vesicles (the bubbles that actually form the image) collapse.

The effects of humidity are dependent partially upon the composition of the base. High humidity eventually causes cellulose acetate to become sticky and the image layer to distort. Polyester is more resistant but eventually degrades if the humidity is accompanied by high heat. Vesicular and diazo emulsions are resistant to the effects of high humidity. Silver halide is very susceptible at humidity levels above 60%. Mold thrives on the gelatin emulsion and hairlike fungal growths will quickly obscure the images.

Dirt and dust abrade the emulsion layer and cause image loss. This is aggravated by packing microfiche too tightly or winding microform too tightly. Particles of dust and scratches will also make reading the images more difficult.

Chemicals and atmospheric pollutants deteriorate the film base as well as causing damage to the image. Silver halide is especially sensitive. Sulfur dioxide, paint fumes, peroxides, ozone, and ammonia are on the list of pollutants that damage silver halide film. Contact with acidic contaminants such as printing inks, rubber bands, boxes, and envelopes cause the emulsion to become soluble and redeposit as red or yellow spots. Even fingerprints are a hazard because the salts carried in perspiration will react with the silver.

Since vesicular images are created by the diffraction of light off tiny bubbles in plastic, they are especially vulnerable to damage from pressure. Equipment malfunctions, pressure from fingernails, or pens and pencils can obliterate the images.

Optimal Conditions For Storage of Film

Despite its frailties, film is an important medium for long-term storage of records. Part of the attraction is that, while it is somewhat fragile, it is easy to duplicate. In practice, most organizations using microfilm store the master film and use only copies. In the case of COM film where there is no master per se, a complete set should be put aside and stored in optimal conditions. This is true of any situation where the organization values the film, does not have the original, and cannot easily or reliably obtain a new copy.

Archival storage conditions are: housing in a separate room or vault; constant, accurate temperature of 70°; constant humidity of 30%; and protection from fire hazards. Protection from excessive dust and pollution is also required. Storage containers should be acid-free.

Microforms: Summed Up

Microfilm is a delicate medium that requires exacting standards and handling. However, we know what those standards and handling practices are. In some ways, because microfilm is more delicate, it is safer because we are aware of, and compensate for, its frailties.

Digital Storage

Information stored by computers differs from that stored on paper and microfilm in a very basic way. Neither film nor paper require a machine to interpret the information stored there. In a pinch, a magnifying glass or a microscope can be used to read microfilm. While machines and technology certainly make it easier to use both paper and microfilm, no machine interprets the symbols on it for us. The educated human mind does that. With magnetic and optical media, the same is not true. Even if you could see the marks made on magnetic or optical disks, they would mean nothing.

This section precedes those on magnetic and optical media because they have many factors in common. The discussion of how information is represented digitally, compression, media layout, and standards apply to both magnetic and optical media. While many people think of magnetic media as storage for encoded data and optical as storage for images, both media can store both types of information.

Representation of Information

Most of the computers in use today are digital computers. They store information that is expressed as combinations of data that are represented by discrete (separate, individual) units. The smallest unit of digital memory is the bit (*binary digit*). The absence or presence of voltage, off/on, represent the 0's and 1's that are the basis of how information is recorded digitally. Eight bits make a byte. Just like any other language, meaning is given to these combinations by agreement. Two of the most common standard codes are ASCII (American Standard Code for Information Interchange) and EBCDIC (Extended Binary Code Decimal Interchange Code). Using ASCII, the alphabet and other standard symbols are represented by a byte. For example, **A** is represented as 11000001. A kilobyte is one thousand bytes, a megabyte is one million-bytes. Optical disk capacity has moved us into giga- and terabyte (billion-and trillion-byte) territory.

Documents stored using a code similar to ASCII require approximately one byte per character of information. This is how information in word processing systems and databases are stored. The program adds some information to give instructions on how to format and output the information (which also takes some storage space). These types of documents are easily changed and revised. However, ASCII representations are limited to the alphabet, numbers, and a few specialized symbols. Codes like ASCII are analogous to Morse Code. Letters and instructions can be represented with these codes but signatures, drawings, graphs, letterheads, etc. cannot be.

Because codes cannot accurately reproduce an image, particularly the handwritten portions, other methods are needed. The two most common methods of storing images digitally are raster and vector. Raster images are bit maps as described below. They describe an image dot by dot. Vector images are more like storing directions to recreate an image in a "connect-the-dots" picture. The information stored gives the direction and duration of the lines to be drawn. Vector images are used primarily by some CAD/CAM (computer-assisted drawing and mapping) systems.

Bit mapping looks at a page and records information by the number of dots per inch (dpi). The number of dots per inch determines the resolution — how accurate and readable the representation is. A bit mapped picture includes every inch of a document. An inch, at 200 dpi, is represented by 200 dots horizontally, multiplied by 200 dots vertically. 40,000 bits are needed to describe the printing or writing on one square inch. Each represents the presence of black or the presence of white. At this resolution, it takes 3,740,000 bits or 467 kilobytes to represent an 8 1/2 by 11 inch document.

$$S = \frac{(H \times R) \times (W \times R)}{8}$$

(S = Storage Requirement in bytes, H = Height of document, W = Width of document, R = DPI)

Increasing either the resolution or the size of the document dramatically increases the number of bytes needed to store the image, as Table 5 illustrates.

At these storage rates, a 60 megabyte disk could store only 128 images (8.5"x11" pages at 200 dpi). To reduce the storage requirements, information is compressed.

Compression

Image Compression

Compression reduces the amount of storage space required for images by the use of algorithms that summarize the sequences and number of dots or pixels. The most popular technique uses run-length encoding. This technique counts the number of successive dots of the same tonality. Instead of storing a whole string of digits to record each of the light spaces across the top margin, a code, to represent the run of light spaces, is stored. Other codes represent runs of varying lengths of a particular tone. Figure 1 is a simplistic representation of how compression works. The actual schemes for data compression are much more complex. There are some standard data compression algorithms. Most widely used are: Modified Huffman coding (the Group III fax machine standard) and modified READ (the Group IV fax machine standard). Modified Huffman is a one-dimensional data compression (horizontal only) technique, while modified READ is two-dimensional (both horizontal and vertical). However, many vendors have their own proprietary compression algorithms which are faster and more efficient. Using proprietary schemes means that compression and decompression can be performed only on the specific equipment and software combination.

Table 5: Storage Required for Bit-Mapped Images (bytes)

DPI	Size of Original		
	8.5 x 11	8.5 x 14	11 x 14.5
150	262,969	334,688	448,594
200	467,500	595,000	797,500
300	1,051,875	1,338,750	1,794,375
400	1,870,000	2,380,000	3,190,000

Figure 1: Simplified Model of Data Compression Run-Length Encoding Method

Not Compressed: white black black black white white white white white white white black white white white white

Compressed: white black^3 white^7 black white^7

Even with compression, storage requirements are tremendous. They are also hard to quantify. There are too many variables to give an easy answer to the question: How many documents will fit on a given piece of media? When a document is bit-mapped, every mark on it is recorded. Individual letters, coffee stains, specks of dust, handwriting, borders on forms, stray pencil marks, logos, charts: all are recorded. The less the contrast between the images and the background, the more information is needed. The amount of white space greatly affects storage requirements. And of course the resolution is a big factor, as is the size of the document.

As you can see from Table 6, a letter-size document may require from 13 to 187 kilobytes of storage.

$$S = \frac{(H \times R) \times (W \times R)}{8} \times \frac{1}{C}$$

S = Storage Requirements by bytes, H = Heights of document, W = Width of document, R = DPI, C = Compression.

The compression factor (a compression factor of 20 means one-twentieth of the space is needed) varies not only with the compression method but from document to document — the fewer the markings and the better the contrast, the smaller the compressed image. An accepted rule of thumb has come to be 40K for an average document scanned at 200 dpi. It is dangerous to size your system on this. "*The average*" document is a poor specification for your specific needs. The best way to determine how much space your documents will require is to scan a sampling of documents and determine a more valid estimate.

Character Compression

Compression of information on disks is not limited to images. There are also schemes that compress the space needed to represent characters. This is important for two reasons: to speed up how fast the information can move from storage into RAM (random access memory) and to reduce the amount of storage needed. Storing information in databases can add a significant performance factor in search times. Compression schemes vary greatly. A simple, but effective, compression technique is to suppress the empty spaces and zeros in data fields. For example, a database with names may have a fixed length field that allows 20 spaces for last names. Without compression *Yu* and *Harrington-Smithers* take up exactly the same amount of space on the disk. By compressing blanks, the storage space for *Yu* is reduced. In a large database, this may make a significant difference in performance. Other compression techniques may reduce storage requirements even more drastically.

Character compression schemes have some drawbacks. Among them is the likelihood that the compression scheme is proprietary. Files can be compressed and decompressed only by the vendor's method. Poorly designed compression schemes can introduce errors into your data. Software compression/decompression also requires processing time, so overall computer system response could decline.

Table 6: Storage Requirements for Compressed Images (in Bytes)

DPI	8.5 x 11	8.5 x 14	14.5 x 11
Compression Factor of 10			
150	26,297	33,469	44,859
200	46,750	59,500	79,750
300	105,188	133,875	179,438
400	187,00	238,000	319,000
Compression Factor of 15			
150	17,531	22,313	29,906
200	31,167	39,667	53,167
300	70,125	89,250	119,625
400	124,667	158,667	212,667
Compression Factor of 20			
150	13,148	16,734	22,430
200	23,375	29,750	39,875
300	52,594	66,938	89,719
400	93,500	119,000	159,500

Physical Layout of Media

When information is read from or written to a storage medium, a read/write head must be sent to the exact location where that information exists and then find all the data in that group of information. How that location is determined and how the read/write head mechanically moves to it has a sharp impact on performance. The time required to access data is a bottleneck. Today's computers are capable of processing information much faster than it can be located and received from tape or disk storage. If more time is spent getting the read/write head aligned with the right place on the storage medium to read the data, the speed (or throughput) is slower. As more data is packed onto media, the degree of precision required to locate the data increases.

The most significant difference in media format is the shape of disks versus tapes and the ability to physically move the read/write head as well as the recording media for disks. This has a very basic inherent limitation on how fast a read/write head can be aligned with a specific place on the storage medium and read the information.

Information is stored sequentially on a tape and the read/write head does not move. If the tape is positioned at the beginning and the desired information is at the end, the entire tape must spool past the read/write head to get to the information. Likewise, if the next desired information is at the beginning, the tape must rewind back to the start to get

the information under the read/write head. Disks allow a greater degree of random access because, the read/write head can be moved physically closer to where the information starts. The read/write head is moved to a different track or location by moving between the outside circumference and center of the disk as the storage medium continues to rotate underneath the head.

Read/write heads must be provided with markers, so they are able to locate information. This is what formatting does. It helps the read/write heads position themselves properly.

Disks

The most common disk format is a series of concentric circles – tracks–cut into wedge-shaped pieces by spokes drawn across the radius of the disk (Figure 2). Each resulting space is called a sector.

This formatting scheme is most often referred to as tracks and sectors. It is also referred to as CAV, constant angular velocity. This refers to the fact that the motor driving the read/write head moves at a constant speed when reading and writing. There are several variants of the CAV scheme. Z-CAV takes advantage of the fact that the outside tracks are longer than the inside tracks by staggering sectors and putting more tracks towards the outside edges (see Figure 2). This scheme increases the storage capacity. CCS, continuous composite servo, disks are etched at the factory with spiral

Figure 2: Disk Formatting Schemes

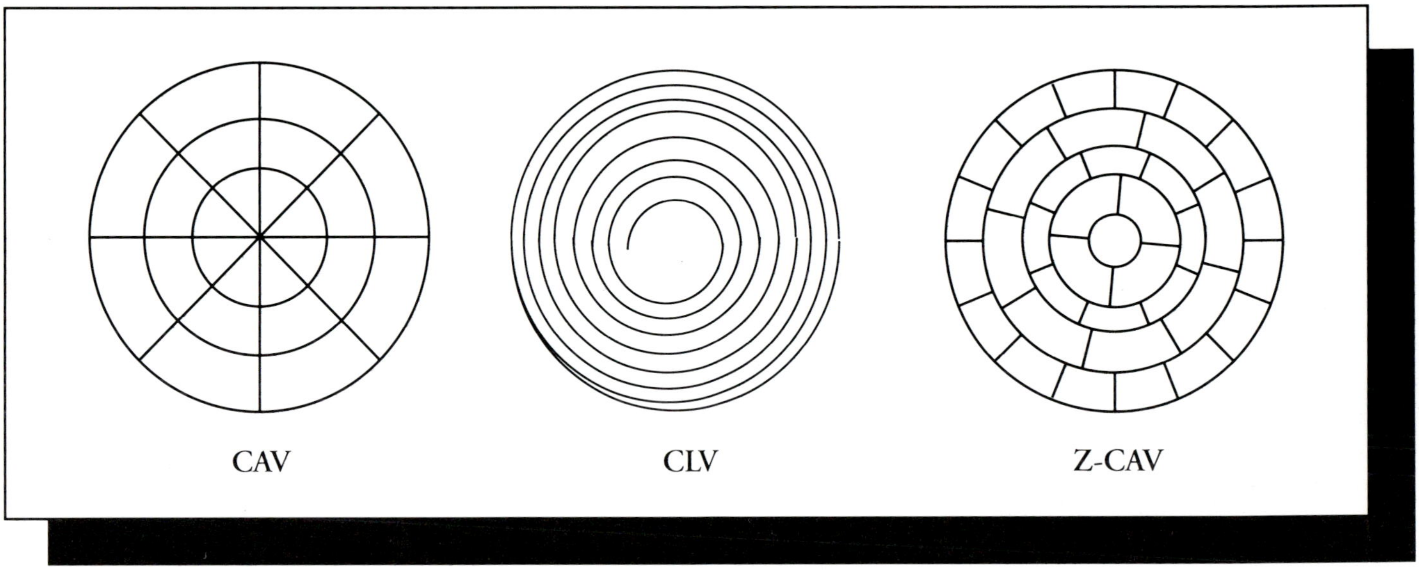

Table 7: Characteristics of Disk Formatting Schemes

CAV	Z-CAV	CCS	SS	CLV
Constant Angular Velocity	Z-Constant Angular Velocity	Continuous Composite Servo	Servo Sampling	Constant Linear Velocity
Standard Disk Rotates at constant speed Very mature technology Widely used for both magnetic and optical disks	Faster access than CAV Potential for more capacity than CAV Some drives read both CAV and Z-CAV Used primarily for optical disks	Standard Disk rotates at constant speed Media is easier to make than SS More mature technology Used for optical disks	Faster access than CCS Very Accurate Tracks faster than CCS Uses only one head vs. three for CCS Used for optical disks	Standard Very wide usage Disk speed varies with positioning of head Used for optical disks, particularly CD-ROM

grooves that define the location of the data tracks. Then three heads read the disk, two read the tracking groove and the other is positioned over the data. SS, servo sampling, is a scheme that stamps disks with regions of precisely calibrated pits that tell the head exactly where the data tracks are. The pits are used to align a single head. More sectors per track are possible and each track is divided into segments. The head is calibrated more than 1400 times in a single rotation of the disk. Speed and accuracy are increased.

CLV, constant linear velocity, disks have information recorded on one long track that spirals from the outer edge to the center (see Figure 2). The head finds the information by its temporal location (addressed by how much time it takes to get to a location. The disk speed must vary, slow down when reading near the center and speed up when reading the outer edge. A disk using this data arrangement reads data sequentially.

Most magnetic disks are formatted using the CAV scheme and compatibility with standards is the norm. CLV is the Standard formatting for CD-ROM (Compact Disk Read Only Memory) disks and some WORM (Write Once Read Many) disks. Z-CAV and SS are not standard. Groups of vendors are promoting and supporting these formats as a way to increase the speed and capacity of optical media. Unless disk drives are designed to accommodate standards or multiple formats, users are limited to certain types of equipment and sources of resupply disks.

Tapes

There are two basic ways of formatting tracks onto tape. The most common method is longitudinal tracks, ones that run the full length of the tape. On tape formatted for helical scan, data is written across the tape in closely spaced diagonal stripes (see Figure 3). Helical scan was developed over thirty-five years ago and has been used extensively in video recording. But it is considered "new" technology because it is now being implemented in tapes with a very high storage density. Helical scan densities can be as much as one hundred times greater than longitudinal tapes.

Figure 3: Helical Scan Tape

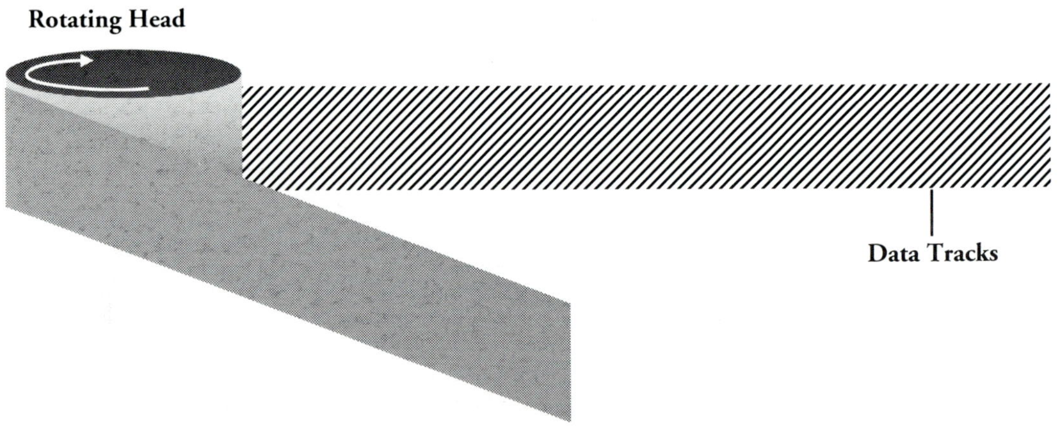

Standards

As can be seen from the discussion above there is often a trade-off between technological advances offering bigger and better (or just different) and what is accepted and commonly used. Standards exist to make systems compatible and to provide measures of acceptability. You can imagine the problems if each paper manufacturer produced whatever size and grades of paper they thought best. Even file cabinets would become obsolete as paper standards changed. Fortunately, as a technology matures, so do its standards. There are a number of agencies, both national and international, that work with manufacturers, researchers, and users to write standards. There is often disagreement as different groups seek to promote the system they prefer, or manufacture.

Standards are important because they offer users consistency, more suppliers, and generally reduced prices. The "best" technology does not always win. When movies were first introduced on videotape, they were competing against movies on laser discs that were far superior in quality. Consumers preferred the tapes because they could also record on them. So a product that was technically superior was not able to compete because buyers were willing to sacrifice superior quality for other considerations. When considering a medium for data storage, the assurance that some one will supply and support the medium in the future is often worth trading-off against the gains in capacity and or speed.

Conclusion

Digital storage involves more than just media. It is inescapably intertwined with the process of accessing and deciphering the information. It involves the hardware that translates the markings on the media to electric impulses, as well as the software that translates those impulses to a format that humans can interpret. If you are recording information to be used at some future date, it will have to be readable at that time. Even if the medium lasts, if the machine and all the software necessary to interpret it are not usable, the information may as well not exist because it will not be accessible.

Magnetic Media
Physical Description

Magnetic media are made of a metallic or plastic base coated with a metallic oxide that can be magnetized. Data is encoded by changing the polarity of small areas of the magnetic coating. The read/write head is an electromagnet that writes by changing the magnetization in a particular area to the proper orientation. The head determines whether an area reads *0* or *1* by the electronic current induced in the head at that area. Tapes are in direct contact with the head. Heads for disks fly on a cushion of air above the rotating disks. Head crashes occur when unwanted physical contact between the head and disk causes damage to the disk.

There are three basic physical types of magnetic media: tape, diskettes, and hard disks. Both tape and diskettes have a flexible polymer base with a coating, usually a ferro-magnetic compound. Tapes are strips of uniform width and are usually enclosed in a plastic cartridge that protects them from dust and fingerprints. Diskettes have jackets for protection of either flexible or rigid plastic. Hard drives are rigid metal or plastic, coated with a metallic film. A single hard drive may have multiple platters attached to a single spindle. Each surface has a read/write head. Hard disks are sealed, sometimes in a removeable pack.

The capacity of magnetic media depends primarily on the metallic coating and the read/write head. A read/write head must be sensitive enough to read the signals produced by the magnetized bits. The strength of the signal depends on the *coercivity* of the metal. Highly coercive metals send a strong signal and need a strong field to reverse polarity. This is very important to packing the bits closer together. If the bits of a material with low coercivity are packed together, a bit may be demagnetized by its neighbor. As more bits are packed into an area, each produces a smaller signal, requiring a head with a very small gap between the poles of its electromagnet. It must be sensitive enough to read a weak signal from a small bit and, at the same time, ignore the signals from neighboring bits. The head must be able to fly very close to the disk; heads that are closer are better able to read weak signals.

Until a few years ago the hard disk was usually a plastic binder sprinkled with slivers of gamma ferric oxide, FE_2O_3. Today most hard disks are coated with a continuous film that is sputtered or plated onto an aluminum drive. The films are pure magnetic materials, the most popular being cobalt nickel alloys. They have a high coercivity and send strong signals. However, they are susceptible to corrosion. Hard carbon coatings protect them from contaminants and damage from the read/write heads. Tapes and diskettes are more exposed to the elements than hard disks, so this type of coating susceptibility to corrosion is ill-suited for those applications. The use of highly coercive materials means the primary limiting factor for magnetic storage on disks is the read/write head.

Most diskettes are either 5.25" inches in diameter or 3.5" in diameter. The smaller disks have a higher capacity because the packaging offers more protection. Higher recording densities are possible. 5.25" diskettes are not as well-protected against the hazards of handling.

Hard drives are well protected. They are sealed in metal or plastic. The size of disk packs for mainframes vary in physical size. The disk drives for a PC are either 5.25" or 3.5". Drive sizes are shrinking (some 2.5" drives are available and more are under development) and their storage capacities are rising.

Early tape drives on mainframe systems used 1/2" reel-to-reel-tapes, which are still used today. With the advent of the PC, quarter-inch tape cartridges (QIC) became popular, first for storage and then for backup. Most mainframe backup evolved to 8-mm tape cartridges. Recently digital audio tape (DAT), has become available. DAT uses digital recording technology and helical scanning to store data on 4-mm tapes. Tapes move across the head more slowly than conventional tapes, but at a much higher rate of data transfer. High-speed movement across the head causes wear and tear plus heat-causing friction which can distort the tape's metal-oxide coating. This distortion can compromise data integrity.

Most tapes do not have to *read* sequentially, as format markings help them find data already written to tape. Recording is a different matter. There are three primary methods of writing information to tape: streaming; random; and update-in-place. Streaming appends data onto a tape. When a file is updated, a new version is added: the old one remains on the tape. Information appears on the tape in the order in which it was recorded. Formatting is done as the tape is written. This is the most common method of access. Random access requires that the tape be preformatted. Selected partitions on the tape can be written over without changing other sections of the tape. The update-in-place method is the newest and most advanced form of random access tape. It is a combination of streaming and random-access. Tapes can both be appended and over-written, but no preformatting is required. Formatting is done on the fly and space for added information is left at set intervals. At this time, most conventional tapes use streaming access. DAT uses both random access and update-in-place.

Table 8: Primary Characteristics of Magnetic Media

Format	Reliability	Capacity	Durability	Speed
Diskette	**Fair** Surface is not smooth and stable enough to allow for heads to fly very close to the surface. Drives have a tendency to get out of alignment.	**Low** Lowest capacity of all magnetic media. Most hold between 360K and 2 megabytes.	**Fair** The durability of diskettes is often in direct proportion to the quality of materials rather than the stresses of use. Diskettes receive more frequent handling and less careful handling than other media.	**Fair** Transfer rates for diskettes are low relative to hard drives. Seek times are generally three times (or more) slower than that of a hard drive.
Hard Disk	**Very Good** Heads can fly very close to media. Can use more coercive metals.	**High** Up to one gigabyte.	**Very Good** Hard drives can be expected to withstand several years of heavy use.	**Excellent** Transfer rates are high and seek time is low.
Conventional Tape	**Fair** Tapes are subject to stress in use that damages the tape and causes loss of data integrity.	**High** Up to 500 megabytes.	**Poor** Not suited for intensive daily use. They wear too quickly.	**Slow** Seek time is slow. Transfer rates are fair.
Digital Audio Tape	**Very Good** Shorter tracks allow for more precision in reading and writing.	**Very High** Up to 1.3 gigabytes per tape.	**Good** Should stand moderate use well, due to reduced stress.	**Very Good** New formatting schemes decrease seek time. Data transfer is fast.

The qualities most desired for magnetic media can be measured by four factors: ability to reliably write and read data, capacity, durability, and speed of access. The ability to write and read data reliably is partially a function of the materials used and the read/write heads, as discussed in the previous section. Reliability also hinges on the data remaining correct after use. Tracking errors, distortion, and errors caused by environmental exposure can reduce reliability. Rigidity and smoothness of disks affect reliability. The closer the head can get to the disk, the fewer the number of read errors. Capacity is a measure of how much information is available at a given time. Durability is how much routine use the media will withstand before wearing out. Speed is determined by how fast the medium can be physically accessed by the computer (seek time) and the information made available to the processor (transfer speed). The reason there are many formats is that you generally get higher quality in one factor by trading it off for lower quality in another. Higher quality in any of the areas is often associated with higher costs. For example, tape is widely used because of its capacity. However, it is rarely on-line and access times are longer. Tape generally wears faster because it is in direct contact with the head and it is wound and rewound, putting stress on the tape.

Storage and Handling

Compared to other media, magnetic media are fragile. Because recording is done by magnetizing metal particles, exposure to strong electrical or magnetic fields can scramble data. Spikes caused by power fluctuations or static electricity have the same effect. High humidity or other exposure to water can corrode metal, plus soften and warp plastic substrates. Smoke, dust, and pollutants attack the substrates and the metal surfaces. Sharp blows may affect the medium. Tapes and hard drives are generally treated with care and respect. Diskettes, on the other hand, are exposed to the constant dangers of the desk top: coffee, jelly doughnuts, paper clips, and other such hazards. They are used as coasters, sent through the mails, x-rayed at airports, and stuffed in shirt pockets. Most survive with data intact. Some do not. Part of the frustration in dealing with magnetic media is that even when it has been pampered and well-cared for, it may get zapped (technical jargon for a major data loss) for no apparent reason. Other times, media can be subjected to severe stresses, even fires and floods, and yet the information can be recovered.

Media used for current data should be backed up to protect it from loss. Most data losses occur during use. Multiple backup copies of important information adds protection. At least one copy should be stored off-site. Then, if your main storage fails and so does the backup, all is not lost.

When data is no longer actively used and changed, it is archived (in data processing terms, that simply means it is no longer accessible on-line). This information is often the only copy, so it should be stored off-site in a temperature and humidity controlled vault. Tapes must be rewound every three to four years to relieve the stresses caused by long-term storage while wound on reels. If information is to be kept for longer periods of time, it must be re-recorded because there is no other way to compensate for the random demagnetization that will occur naturally even under the best storage conditions.

State of the Art and Advances

Rapid advances are being made in magnetic storage technology. Capacities of both tape and disk are increasing. Two notable advances are being made in the area of floppy disks. One is the *floptical.* It is a barium-ferrite, BaFe, 3.5" magnetic disk with about 800 concentric grooves embossed on it. The head uses optics to track its position on these grooves and magnetism to record and write in the space between. Due to the increased track density, flopticals store about 20 megabytes per disk. Drives are the same size as a standard 1-inch high, 3.5" floppy drive. Drives have two heads so they can also read and write standard floppies. Another recent innovation is perpendicular recording using barium ferrite. With this technology the medium is magnetized vertically rather than horizontally or parallel to the recording surface. This allows for higher densities and increased transfer rates. Currently the disk capacity is 4 megabytes, but improved drives will allow for 32 megabytes per disk in the next few years.

Advances in head technology continue to push the limits of magnetic media. Prototypes that can store as many as 1.8 million bits per square millimeter have been made, which compares well to WORM disks.

Optical Media

Optical media, in and of itself, only provides new materials and equipment for recording information we already have the capability to store. Anything that can be stored on optical disk can be stored in magnetic memory. The *optical* in optical media refers to how the information is recorded and read. A laser is the key. A laser beam is a beam of intense light that is amplified and moves together on the same wavelength. This coherent light can be focused on a very narrow area and used to leave a mark or read one by measuring the change in reflection or refraction. Magnetic media uses changes in magnetization to record the 0's and 1's understood by digital computers. Optical media changes how light is reflected or refracted, usually by making small pricks, bubbles, or burns in a special material.

Physical Description and Recording Methods
CD-ROM Disks

CD-ROM is familiar to many people as a medium for recorded music. The same medium is also used to store data. The CD-ROM is a plastic (polycarbonate) disk sandwich with an outer diameter of 120 mm, an inner diameter of 15 mm, and a thickness of 1.2 mm. It is made by pressing soft plastic against a master disk mold, then coating it with a shiny aluminum layer that follows the bumps and smooth areas on the plastic base. The aluminum is then coated with a layer of tough protective lacquer. A CD-ROM has a capacity of 540 megabytes of digital information. Data is stamped onto the disk from the master and cannot be added or deleted. Data is laid on one continuous track over three miles long. Because the disk must rotate at varying speeds, access times are from 350 to 600 milliseconds, as opposed to 30 milliseconds or less for magnetic hard drives. To locate information on a CD-ROM, the index is searched for an address for the data. Then the read head moves to the approximate location. The rotational speed of the disk slows down or speeds up, as needed, to the correct speed for reading in that area of the disk. Next a bit of information is read. Using that, the precise location is determined, and the head shifted to the correct address. Due to the complexity of this operation, it is not even theoretically possible that CD-ROM access speeds will ever come close to the speed of today's magnetic hard drives. CD-ROM disks adhere to standards for both physical dimensions and directory structure. This means any CD-ROM can be read by any manufacturer's CD-ROM drive.

WORM Disks

WORM disks are not as standard as CD-ROM disks. They come in a variety of sizes: 3.5 inches, 4.72 inches, 5.25 inches, 8 inches, 10 inches, 12 inches, and 14 inches. The 5.25 inch disks are the most common. The 12 and 14 inch disks are battling for dominance in the big disk market. The whole area will benefit when standards are in place. Disks are made of rigid plastic and are usually encased in a plastic shell. Protected by the plastic shell is a recording surface, most commonly a thin film of rare earth metal, but it can also be an organic film. The primary criterion is that the surface can be changed permanently in a way that will measurably change how light passes through the surface. Most disks pit a metal surface by burning holes into it or popping preformed bubbles. Some use dye polymer recording which uses light to change the color, and therefore the optical properties, of an organic film.

Read/write heads for WORM disks are bulky, making access times slower than for magnetic disk. They also require more power. WORM disks, as their name implies, can be written on once, and then cannot be changed.

Magneto-Optical

Similar to flopticals, magneto-optical (MO) technology combines magnetic and optical technologies. The disks are built from layers of materials. From the bottom up: the substrate is glass or plastic etched with grooves and format markers; a dielectric layer that enhances the effects of the read laser, the recording layer made of a rare-earth transition-metal alloy; another dielectric layer; and a protective layer. The recording layer of an MO disk is always magnetized. The surface affects the polarization of light that reflects off of it by rotating the polarization. Depending on the surface charge, the light will rotate either clockwise or counterclockwise. This is called the Kerr effect. The information on the disk is read by the changes in Kerr rotation of a low-power laser beam.

Writing to an MO disk means changing the magnetic orientation of one spot without disturbing neighboring spots. This is accomplished with a high-powered write-laser. The laser heats the spot to its curie point, the point at which magnetic substances lose their magnetic orientation, and then a small electromagnet generates a magnetic field that reflects the new orientation of the spot. As the spot cools, it assumes this orientation.

Figure 4: Reading and Writing to an MO Disk

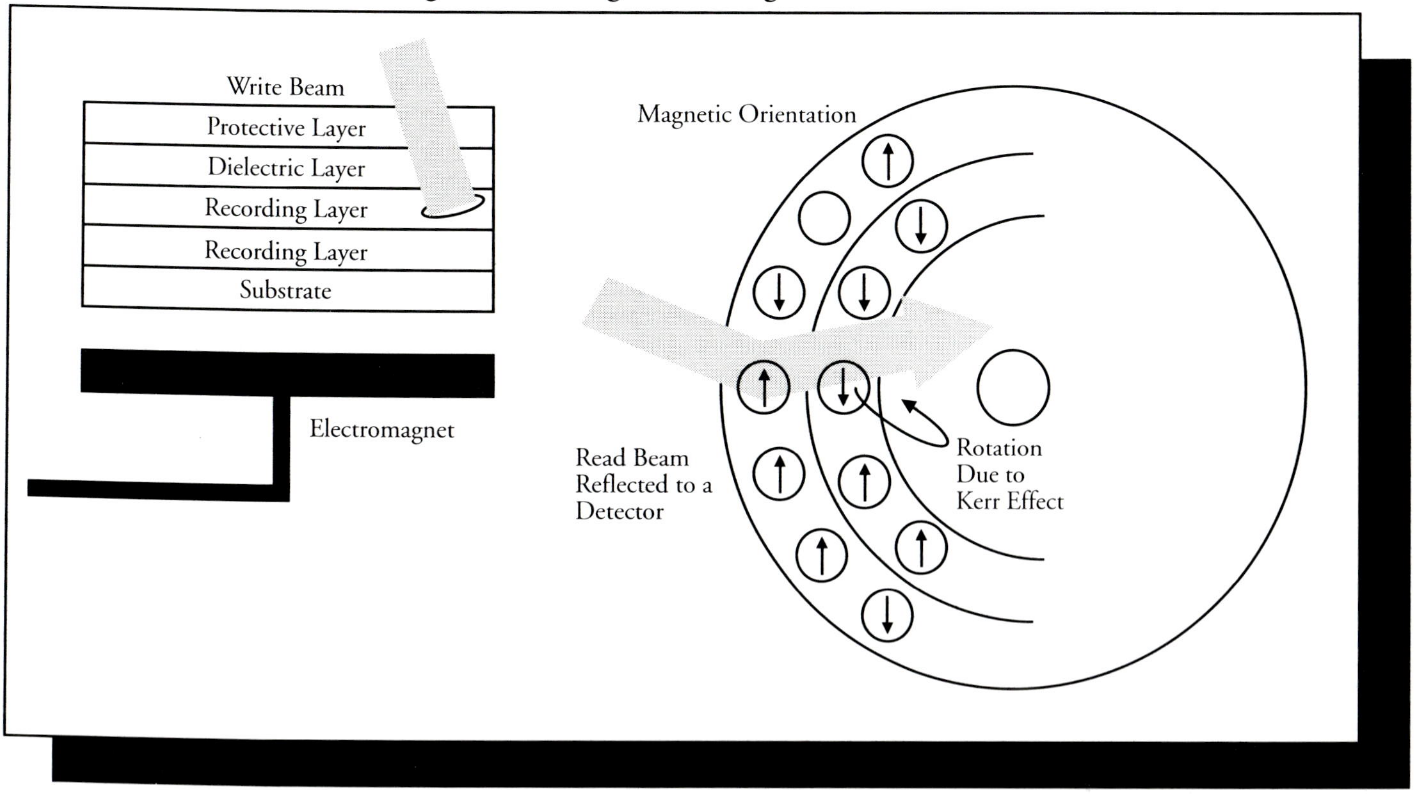

When an MO disk is manufactured, all the spots on the disk have the same orientation, the default. When the drive writes to the disk, it assumes the default. Therefore, it must erase the area (bring it back to default) before it writes on it. This doubles the time needed to write to the disk. Other limitations involve the read/write heads. The magnitude of the Kerr rotation is small — about 1% — so the head needs relatively large optics to detect the changes. A massive head has to move slower. The result is that magnetic drives are two to four times faster than MO drives. An MO drive is also as much as six times slower in accessing a particular spot on the disk. The 35 to 100 milliseconds seek time is as much as six times slower than a magnetic disk, but compares well to the 25 to 40 seconds required for most tape formats.

All the MO disks that are currently available are 5.25" in diameter. The intrinsic signal quality in MO systems is not as good as for write-once systems. This means the data density is lower, as are the data transfer rates (average is about 1megabyte per second). Disks that are currently available range in capacity from about 600 megabytes to over 2 gigabytes.

Phase-Change

Another rewriteable disk technology uses the purely optical properties of phase change. Phase change disks are based on the ability of a category of thin films (semimetal materials that can be deposited onto a substrate in a very thin film) that are able to switch between two stable structural states. The thin films used in phase change are based on tellurium or selenium. They can exist in both an amorphous and a crystalline state. The important aspect of this is that the two different states reflect light differently, a difference that can be read and interpreted as data.

Phase change disks are built in layers, much like MO disks. There is a substrate, a layer to enhance reflective contrast, the thin film recording layer, another layer to enhance reflective contrast, and a protective layer on top. The origi-

Figure 5: Phase Change Reading and Writing

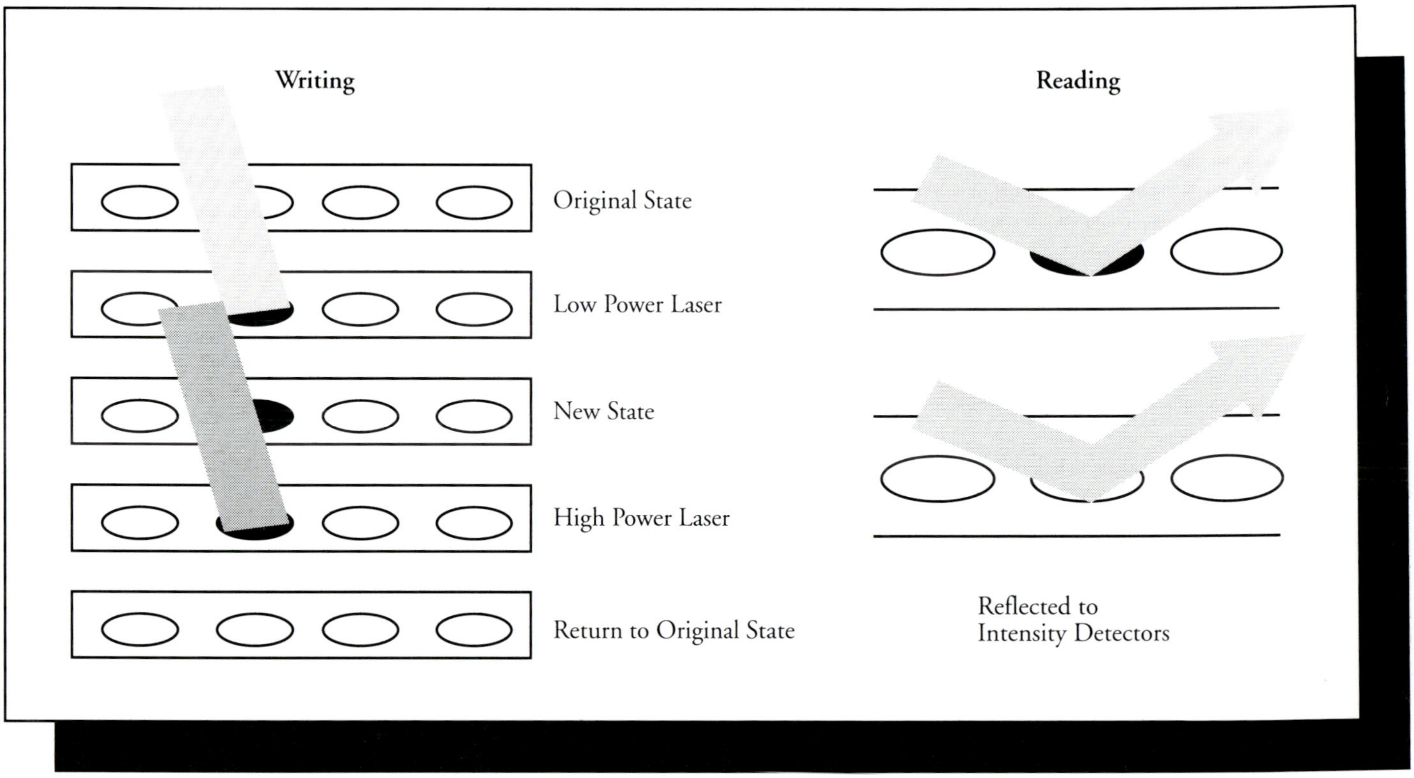

Writing

- Original State
- Low Power Laser
- New State
- High Power Laser
- Return to Original State

Reading

Reflected to Intensity Detectors

nal state of all the spots in the recording layer is amorphous. When a low-powered laser heats a spot, it changes to a crystalline state. A higher powered laser zaps the same spot and melts it. When the spot cools it is amorphous. This ability to switch states without going back to neutral (like MO disks) eliminates the separate erasing step.

Currently only one manufacturer has shipped phase change disks, but more are planning to. The disk currently available is 5.25" and has a capacity of 940 megabytes. The average seek time is 90 milliseconds and the average transfer rate is 10.3 megabytes per second. The seek time is about the same as the average MO disk and three to six times longer than for hard disks.

Digital Paper

Ninety-eight percent of all optical systems are disk-based at this time. That may change. Optical tape and optical cards (plastic cards the size of credit-cards) will have some applications for records managers. More likely to impact records storage is digital paper. It is made of dye polymer optical recording material coated onto a polymer substrate. It is cheap and flexible (physically). That means it can be cut into strips and wound like a tape. Information is stored by changing the dyes in the optical coating to reflect light differently. Digital paper can be used as cards, tape, or optical floppy disks.

One of the first applications of digital paper was as a backup tape system. Each tape has a capacity of one terabyte, about the same as 5,000 conventional magnetic tape cartridges. The tapes are 800 meters long by 35 mm wide and fit on a 12.5 inch open reel. Average access time is under 30 seconds. The tape is much thicker than magnetic tape, so it is far more resistant to wear and can be wound and rewound much faster.

Digital paper is also being used in Bernoulli drives. 5.25" disks of optical paper, with two disks per cartridge, yield a capacity of 1.2 gigabytes of formatted storage. Average access time is about 56 milliseconds. The disk drives use standard Bernoulli drive technology and cartridge sizes. The head is small and light. The digital paper Bernoulli disk offers the advantages of a light-weight system.

Life Expectancy of Optical Media

Many grandiose claims have been made about how rugged and durable optical disks are. Optical media are fairly rugged and tolerate a greater variance in environment than microfilm and magnetic media. But they are not indestructible.

Optical media must satisfy many constraints — optical, magnetic, mechanical, thermal, metallurgical, and so on. Optical media incorporate a wide variety of materials, designs, and manufacturing techniques. So there are a number of ways for optical media to fail.

- *Mechanical failure.* High temperatures and humidity can affect the plastic substrate, causing it to warp and increasing the number of read/write errors.

- *Optical efficiency.* Any changes in the recording layers or substrate that alter the optical constants can also alter the reflectance and affect both the recording sensitivity or

reduce the readout. The materials themselves do not necessarily change. Scratches, dust, and other contaminants can obscure a transparent substrate. One office installed an optical disk imaging system. After a few months of successful performance, they experienced repeated errors both in recording new images and reading old ones. They finally discovered that the fan on the optical drive pulled air over the disk. The new system had been installed in newly carpeted offices. The disk became coated with dust and oily carpet fibers. After the disks were cleaned, the read/write problems subsided.

- *Recording performance.* Recording relies heavily on the physical and chemical properties of the recording layers. Changes such as corrosion, cracking, or crystallization can result in lost information or problems in recording.

Table 9: Optical Formats and Capacities

Type	Size	Capacity (MB)[1]	Access Time	Cost/MB[2]
CD-ROM	4.8 inches	550	300-600 ms	1-10¢
WORM	5.25 inches	240-1,200	75 ms	25-60¢
WORM	12 inches	1,000-2,000	150 ms	25-40¢
MO Disk	5.25 inches	240-1,000	35-100 ms	25-40¢
Phase Change	5.25	940	90 ms	n/a
Optical Tape	12.5 inch reel	1,000,000	30 sec	1¢
Digital Paper Disk	5.25 inches	1,200	56 ms	6¢

[1]*Where capacity varies, the largest available capacity is shown as capacities are increasing very quickly.*

[2]*Cost figures change rapidly and also depend greatly on quantity. Use these numbers for general comparison only!*

- *Data retention.* Markings make a physical or chemical change to a recording layer, so the stability of the marks or pits may differ from the unrecorded portion. Pits in ablative write-once media can become clogged or obscured by debris generated during subsequent recording.

- *Error rate.* The defect level is usually the most sensitive to harsh environmental conditions. Small localized defects caused by film cracking, delamination, or corrosion may not cause problems with overall signal strength or reflectance, but it may cause localized error bursts that will grow longer because the damage spreads with age and use. Due to the error correction schemes incorporated within many applications, damage might be catastrophic before any external indication is available to the user.

Most makers of optical disk guarantee data retention for ten years. A few have even gone so far as to guarantee data integrity for fifty years. However, if your disk fails you will get only a new disk — no help in restoring data or compensation for lost data.

The difficulty with determining the life of an optical disk is that the technology is new and involves far more than just the length of time the raw materials will last. Ten years is a fairly safe estimate for the lifespan of most optical media. Just as with any other media, this lifespan cannot be taken for granted.

The durability of optical disk images encompasses more than simply how long the information will remain on the disk. The information on the disk is useless without the ability to locate the image data on the disk and translate that data into a screen or printed replica. In addition to the equipment needed, the software interface is critical. While there are some standards, most software is proprietary. The hardware and software combination to read optical disks are unique to most systems. Rapid improvements are being made to both software and hardware. Some vendors believe that having a technical edge is better than adhering to a standard. They often believe they are setting new standards. Sometimes they are. There is no guarantee that new equipment will read old disks. The technology is so new and is advancing so rapidly that some formats and disk sizes are destined for obsolescence (of course, we don't know which

ones just yet). The "safest" disk size is 5.25". It is the most common and the one under the most intensive development.

Handling Requirements

Dust, light, heat, and humidity in the normal office ranges usually have no adverse effects on optical disks. Special handling and storage are not required. However, abusive handling can cause damage. The damage may not be noticeable initially, but it can spread.

Optical paper requires more care in handling because it is a polymer. The normal range of office environments pose no problems. Intense heat and humidity, however, will degrade the polymer base.

Table 10 summarizes the ANSI standards for 130-mm (5.25 inch) WORM disks. These standards apply equally well to CD-ROM. MO disks are very resistant to magnetism, but intense fields could cause damage. Disks and digital paper that have a polymer base are more sensitive to light and to extremes and fluctuations in, heat and humidity. Phase change disks may also be vulnerable to intense, prolonged heat.

State of the Art and Advances

Optical recording technology is in its infancy. There are many advances and improvements to be made. New and improved materials and techniques will help increase storage capacity and reduce access times. Advances in particular are expected in the area of rewriteable disks (especially 3.5" disks), expanded uses of digital paper, and dye-polymer recording.

Holostore

Methods of storing digital data in 3-D (three dimensional) holograms are being developed. Holostore offers the possibility of extremely fast, nonvolatile, high capacity storage. Prototypes are expected to be less than 2" by 2" by .5" in size with a capacity between 200 megabytes and 2 gigabytes with the ability to transfer between 100 and 800 megabytes per second. Achievable targets are capacities of 100 gigabytes with a transfer rate of over 1 terabyte per second. A top-of-the-line disk drive can only transfer 3 to 8 megabytes per second. Holostore will essentially eliminate the bottleneck between processors and storage. The performance factors

Table 10: Environmental Restrictions for 5.25" WORM Disks ANSI 1987

Parameters	Operation[1]	Storage	Shipping[2]
Temperature (° F)	50 to 122	14 to 122	-4 to 131
Relative Humidity (%)	10 to 80	10 to 90	5 to 90
Temperature Gradient	50	59	68
General	No condensation on or in the disk Wet bulb temperature no more than 82° F[3] Temperature RH gradient less than 50° F/Hr. Air pressure from 0.75 to 1.05 bars[4] Air class 1,000,000[5] At least 2 hours of conditioning prior to operation[6]		

[1] *Temperatures in sealed drive enclosures and heat dissipated from system components could easily raise temperatures and cause frequent temperature cycling through a wide range.*

[2] *Shipping conditions are meant to have a duration of only 14 days and reflect the conditions that might be encountered in shipment by truck or train.*

[3] *The absolute amount of moisture corresponding to the amount that would saturate the air at 82° F.*

[4] *High pressure may cause some disk designs which have sealed air layer or pocket to warp or split open the disk.*

[5] *This refers to the number of particles per cubic foot of air that are larger than 0.5mm in diameter.*

[6] *The conditioning requirements help cushion shock from extreme changes aand maintain the requirement of no condensation.*

could increase by a thousand. Holostore will most likely appear first as a special memory device and cache controller. It would sit between the processor and disk or tape storage. The data/program files in use would be loaded into holstore and be instantly accessible to the processor. Changes would be written to the holostore device and subsequently back to the storage medium. Since holostore is non-volatile, the data is not lost when the computer is turned off.

Comparison: Physical Features

Table 11 is a matrix that compares some of the characteristics of each medium. This matrix is only a guideline to the relative differences in the media. The actual numbers may vary greatly depending on the actual equipment and media format used.

Capacity

Capacity has to be measured in two very different ways, depending on whether the representation of the information is encoded and/or a replication of an image. (See the discussion on representation of information.)

Units Required To Store 50,000 Pages

This shows how many units of a given media and format are required to store 50,000 pages. These figures are based on capacities that may change very rapidly for optical disk. The sections on representation of information and compression explain how to make a more accurate estimate of capacities for a specific situation.

Retrieval Speed

This is how quickly the records can be retrieved from storage and passed to the user.

Reusability of Information

The ability to sort, select, and/or revise information to use in creating new documents.

Availability

Availability measures how many people can have access to identical information. Paper scores low on this point because of the difficulty in keeping extra copies of records updated. The ability to completely replace old information with inexpensive new copies increases availability.

File Integrity

File integrity is the ability to consistently find a complete, current copy of a record in the expected location.

Ease of Adding New Files

This measures the ease of adding new information that does not have to be interfiled with other information.

Ease of Updating Current Files

This measures the ease of either replacing or interfiling new information with old information.

Life Expectancy of Media And Information

The length of time the record copy of a document stored on a given medium can reasonably be expected to last. For paper, the record copy is usually the working copy as well. Microfilm almost always has, or should have, an archival copy that is stored under optimal conditions and not used.

Shipping Costs

The cost of physically moving documents a long distance. It is directly related to the bulk and weight of the medium.

Number of Images Per Cubic Foot

A comparison of the number of images that can be stored on the medium that can be stored in one cubic foot of space. Again, this is a general comparison. Specific systems will differ.

Handling Control

This is a measure of how safe records are when they are being handled and the ability to exercise control over the documents. Probably the greatest danger to paper is the chance of loss during handling: spilled coffee; original-eating copy machines; being filed with the wrong group of documents; being discarded inadvertently; etc.

Environmental Resistance

This compares environmental resistance. A medium with a high rating requires fewer environmental controls.

Disaster Resistance

This is a measure of the ability to recover from a catastrophe: fire, floods, severe weather exposure, power outages, etc. It also takes into account the ease with which duplicate or backup copies are made and stored elsewhere.

Equipment Costs

Some media cannot be used without special equipment, so the cost range of equipment must be part of the comparison.

Cost of Media

This is a cost that is subject to frequent change. It is a general cost comparison of what was available at a given point in time for a specific format.

Copyability

Copying records entails more than simply the cost of materials. In most cases the material costs either the same, or close to, the cost for the original. The ease of operating the copying equipment, the time involved, and the routine access to equipment to make the copies determine how copyable a medium is. A high rating means that copies are relatively quick and easy to make.

Table 11: Comparison of Media–Physical Characteristics

	Paper[1]	Microfilm[2]	Magnetic[3]	Optical[4]
Capacity[5] Images	Two images per page. Requires about 40 KB per side to digitize.	100 ft roll 2800 215 ft roll 6336 Fiche 98 COM 420	1.4 MB 350 40 MB 10,000 60 MB 15,000 120 MB 30,000 600 MB 150,000	CD-ROM 13,750 WORM 5.25" 5,000 WORM 12" 25,000 MO 5.25" 16,250
Capacity Encoded	About 4 KB per side	N/A	1.4 MB 35 40 MB 1,000 60 MB 1,500 120 MB 3,000 600 MB 15,000	CD-ROM 137,500 WORM 5.25" 50,000 WORM 12" 250,000 MO 5.25" 16,250
Units Required To Store 50,000 Pages	Three, four drawer file cabinets	17.4 100 ft rolls 7.9 215 ft rolls 510 Fiche 119 COM Fiche	N/A	CD-ROM 3.6 WORM 5.25" 10.0 WORM 12" 2.0 MO 5.25" 3.0
Retrieval Speed	Poor Measured in minutes, hours, and even days before requested information is available.	Poor to Good Ease depends on format and indexing method. Usually found in under 15 minutes.	Excellent Hard Disk 28 - 14 ms Tape 3.5 - 36 sec[6] Faster access than optical, but less on-line.	Excellent CD-ROM 300-600 ms WORM 5.25" 75 ms WORM 12" 150 ms MO 5.25" 35-100 ms Slower than magnetic, but more on-line.
Reusability of Information	None	None	Excellent	Excellent—if encoded data
Availability of Same Document To Multiple Users	Very Poor Can use copy, but no assurance it is complete & latest copy.	Very Good Accurate copies can be made quickly and inexpensively.	Superb Access is limited only by equipment, which is standard and available to many workers.	Excellent Access is limited by special equipment, but accurate copies can be made quickly and inexpensively.
File Integrity	Poor	Excellent	Good Tends to be short-term and subject to loss.	Excellent
Ease of Adding New Files	Excellent	Excellent	Excellent	Excellent
Ease of Updating Current Files	Excellent	Poor	Excellent	Fair to Excellent Must plan well so will not span too many disks.

	Paper	Microfilm	Magnetic	Optical
Life Expectancy of Media and Information	Under 50 years. Can be several hundred.	200-300 yrs. for archival film.	Several years with very careful handling.	Probably 10 years, possibly 50. Unproven.
Shipping Costs	Expensive Bulky and heavy. Weight between 22 and 35 lbs per cubic foot.	Inexpensive Microfilm not bulky or heavy	Moderate to Expensive Magnetic media not heavy, but bulky. Requires special handling or high cost transmission.	Very Inexpensive Very low weight and bulk.
Number of Images Per Cubic Foot	2,000 - 4,000	Roll/100 270,000 Roll/215 580,000 Fiche 705,600 COM 63,000,000	N/A	CD-ROM 1,375,000 WORM 5.25" 500,000 WORM 12" 1,250,000 MO 5.25" 1,625,000
Handling Control	Weak Easy to misplace or lose.	Fair Usually requires a central location.	Excellent Can be routed electronically.	Good to Excellent Can be routed electronically.
Environmental Resistance	Fair Controlled environment required for longevity.	Poor Susceptible to humidity, temperature, dust, and pollutants.	Poor Susceptible to temperature, magnetic fields, power fluctuations, dust, and pollutants.	Very Good Most rugged of media, but not invulnerable.
Disaster Resistance	Low Vulnerable to water and fire.	Excellent Not resistant but easy and routine to keep a copy in storage.	Poor to Fair Usually backups are kept, but some data may be lost. Unless centrally administered, back-ups may be inconsistent.	Fair Relatively resistant, copies easily. Backup should be part of creation process.
Equipment Costs	None to Medium	Low to High	Medium to Very High	High to Very High
Cost of Media Per Image	1.5 to 5¢ per sheet of paper	1/2¢ per page or less	Hard Drives 16-40¢ Floppy 8¢	CD-ROM 0.4¢ WORM 5.25" 3.0¢ WORM 12" 0.6¢ MO 5.5" 1.5¢
Copyability	Fair	Excellent	Poor to Fair	CD-ROM Very Good Other Poor to Fair

[1] Figures are given for letter-sized documents.

[2] Figures given for 24x reduction on rolls and fiche. Fiche numbers are for 98 frame fiche and 420 frames for COM fiche.

[3] Except where otherwise noted, magnetic media storage, and capacities are expressed for encoded information rather than images.

[4] Except where otherwise noted, optical media capacities are shown for images. No figures are given for optical tape as it is not, as of yet, being used in an imaging system.

[5] Scanning resolution of 200 DPI with a compression factor of 10.

[6] For most widely used tapes.

Section 3: Fundamental Differences in Records

Applying technology to solve records mangement problems is a good idea as long as it is understood that technology is not a substitute for management. Failing to understand the fundamental differences in records is far more likely to result in a poor system than choosing the 5.25 inch drives over 3.5 inch drives or microfilm over optical disk.

Records have various functional purposes. The value of records is determined by their functional purpose, operational value, and age. If these differences are not recognized, the records management system may have flaws that changes in technology and medium can not compensate for. Poorly conceived solutions can create more problems.

Treating all records alike is a formula for failure. In our search for consistency and control, we can lose sight of the real reasons for a record to exist and the reason for keeping it. Understanding the differing roles of records means recognizing that the best solution may be a set of complementary systems rather than a one-size-fits-all answer. It also means recognizing that as records pass from active to inactive to storage, the management requirements change.

Inherent Functional Differences

Each of the four types of records: relational data, draft data, documents, and publications serves a fundamentally different purpose. If these differences are ignored, there may be an underlying flaw in the records systems designed to manage them. These inherent differences also mean a reasonable application of technology for one type of information can be inappropriate for another.

A fundamental difference between *documents* and other types of records is the treatment of old information. Documents provide a historical record, a snapshot of conditions at a given point in time. Documents may be thrown out when they are not needed, but they are not replaced by new records. A copy of your latest personnel action adds to your file, it does not replace the previous action. An old contract is not thrown out when a new one is written. Documents are discarded when information about the actions they record is no longer of any value. The information does not wear out, only the need for it.

Table 12: Basic Categories of Records

	Relational	Draft	Documents	Publications
Definition	Discrete pieces of information that are linked together to form a record. Usually a database.	Working copies used in the process of approval and/or revision.	Prove that an action has been taken. After authentication, it should not be altered.	Information intended for an outside audience. Can include regulations, forms, catalogs, periodicals, manuals, etc.
Primary Purpose of Records	Provide current information quickly and accurately. **The latest and greatest.**	Reusing stored drafts can save time, plus improve quality, by serving as the basis for new documents. **Spare parts inventory.**	A history of the decisions and actions taken by action taken by the organization. **Picture of given point in time.**	Get to audience on time while copying and distribution costs stay proportional to the value of the information. **Look it up.**

Records in the other three categories are replaced by new versions of information. Old copies of relational information and drafts should serve one purpose, the ability to rebuild the current copy in the event of loss. Once they are superseded, obsolete, or no longer needed for reference, no reason exists to keep outdated publications.

Part of the difficulty in managing records is that the same *information* often exists as more than one *record* type. For example, an agency may make a policy decision and then publish a regulation to implement it. Three categories of records are created: a draft; a document; and a publication.

- Those records that show the history of the decision-making process and its final results are documents. Records of review and approval are especially important.

- Draft copies of an older regulation are sometimes used to create a new draft of the regulation. The biggest mistake made with drafts is to mark-up copies which already serve as a record of a decision. Drafts are *not* documents. Recordkeeping practices that preserve them as such have a fundamental flaw.

- After the approval process is over, the decision and methods of implementation need to be available to those affected. This involves copying (or publication) and distribution.

Duplicate records are not necessarily a problem. Because duplication is often a symptom of a problem, controlling duplication often becomes a goal. We can go too far. A copy of the publication may be kept in draft format, the original in another file, and extra copies of the publication in a stock room. In this case, anyone who tries to design a system to eliminate all but one copy fails to realize that each version of the record has a fundamentally different purpose. Planned, limited duplication has a positive role in the management of records.

Trying to manage information by content rather than function creates problems that are difficult to compensate for. On the surface it may appear simpler and more efficient to focus on the relationship of various records and to keep, and treat, related information alike. In the short term, this strategy can be successful. In the long term, as information is needed for evidentiary purposes or the issues of long term storage arise, the strategy fails. While all of the records created in the example above have short-term value, only the documents need to be preserved. Preserving multiple copies of outdated publications strains the capacity of the system. Preserving drafts on floppy disk as a historical record focuses on protecting the wrong type of information. This inappropriate focus may also mean that the documentation is incomplete. If we rely on the drafts or copies of the publication to document the decision, the records may not be complete. We begin keeping too much of the wrong type of records to compensate for not keeping the right type of records.

Underlying Records Structure

The basic records structures (unit, transaction, and reference) have already been defined in the introduction. These underlying structures prescribe the basic organization of the records. The basis for differentiation is the determination of when records are no longer active. New information is added to active records. Inactive records may be kept, but new information is not added after closing the record. Any information created after the closing date is stored with different set of records. For example, at the end of the fiscal year, new accounting records are made. The records from the previous year are closed.

- Transactional records are structured by date. Their life span is predictable and consistent. The activity level for records of a given age is also relatively predictable. Records are kept active for a given period of time and then closed. Records with the same date of *creation* can be managed (closed, transferred, retired, destroyed) as a group.

- Unitized records depend upon the occurrence of an event whose date cannot be predicted. Records are active until this event occurs. Once the event occurs, the record is closed. No new information is added after the *closing* date. Records are transferred, retired, and purged as a group by their closing date. For example, old personnel records are purged by the date of severance, not the date someone was hired. This record structure keeps related information together and helps prevent its premature disposal. (There is a vast difference between keeping a record for 10 years and keeping it for 10 years *after* someone retires.)

Table 13: Primary Records Function and Underlying Structure

	Primary Function			
Structure	Relational	Draft	Document	Publication
Unit Records that group all information related to an individual, organization, or activity. Records are closed based on an event rather than a fixed date.	Must be handled differently than most relational information. Purging by events rather than fixed dates. More difficult to manage than transactional records.		Most common purpose of unitized records is to document events, actions, and decisions for one case, individual, or project.	
Transaction Chronological history of events. Value diminishes predictably with age. Records are retired based on creation date.	Good for computerized relational systems. Most relational information is on current events, good for reports compiling and extracting information.		Even if important transactions are recorded and compiled relationally, supporting documentation exists as well.	
Reference Reference information kept until replaced with an update, supplanted by a different record, or is obsolete.	Relational databases structured as reference records. Update information as it changes. More difficult to maintain than transactional.	Draft documents should be structured as reference records. Keep draft copies only to "recycle" or use for information, then discarded.		Publications must be kept as reference records. Not all reference records are publications. A Rolodex of addresses is kept as a reference, but is not a publication.

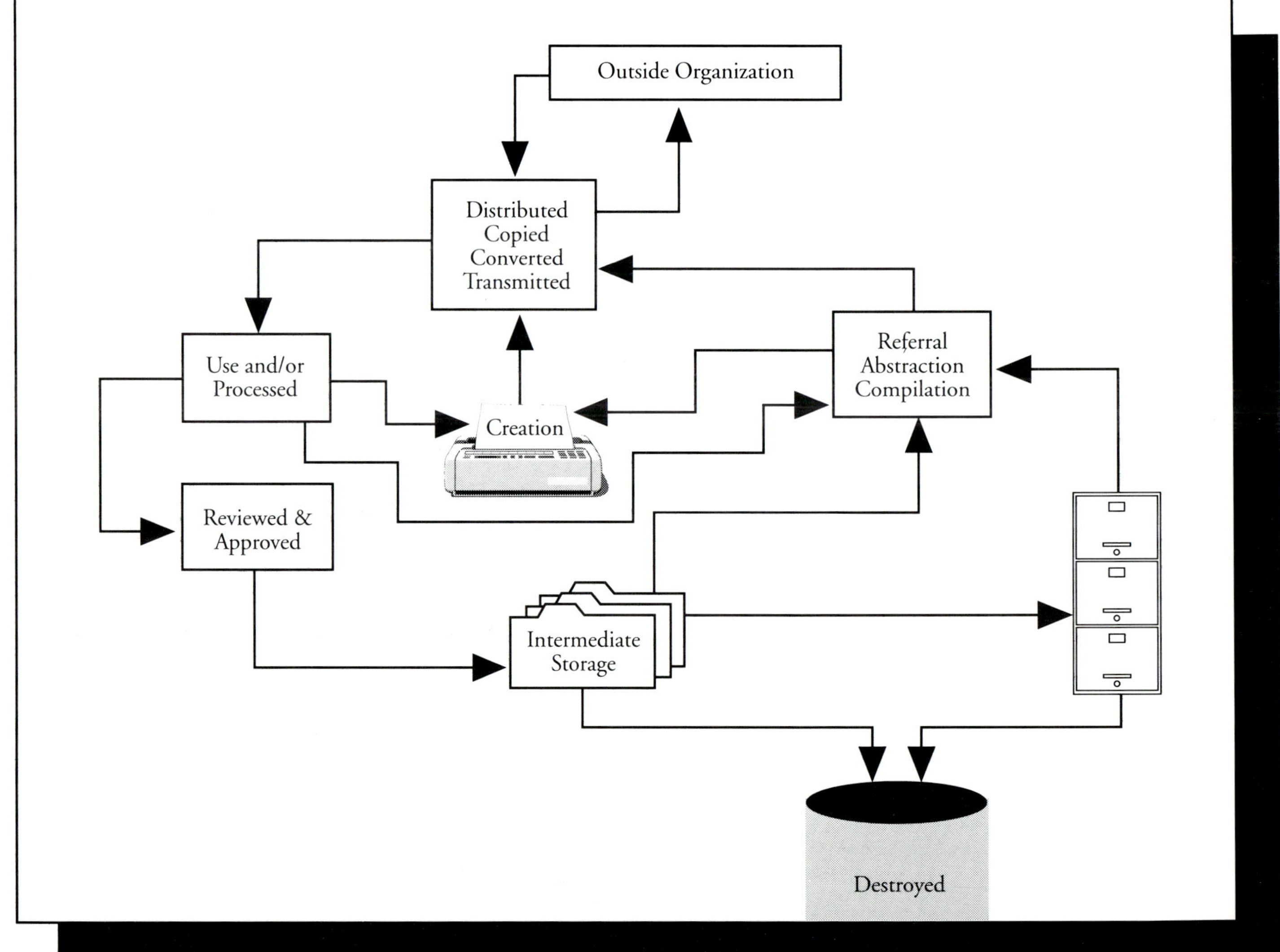

- Reference records differ from the other two types of records because they are kept only while active. Once reference information no longer applies, it should be destroyed. Manuals for a system no longer owned, for example, should be discarded — not stored. Destruction decisions are made on a document by document basis.

Basic records structure is often confused with arrangement (alphabetical, numerical, chronological, etc.) Records structure is *dictated* by the underlying nature and function of the information. Arrangement is a choice. Transactional records may be arranged by name, number, location, but regardless of the arrangement, old files are closed at the end of the filing period and new ones created for the next. One year is the most common filing period, but it can be a week, a month, a quarter, or every six months. Table 13 shows the juxtaposition of structure and primary function.

Time Related Differences: The Record Life Cycle

All records are not created equal, and their value fluctuates with time and circumstance. A quarterly activity report written six months ago may never be used again. An invoice that was paid fourteen months ago and has been languishing in the files, is suddenly crucial to resolving a payment dispute.

Figure 6 illustrates the concept of a life cycle for records. While this model is most often associated with documents, it holds true for relational information, drafts, and publications as well. Each type of record has its own distinct lifecycle.

Records are born, reproduced (some of them many, many times), processed, consulted, reviewed, sent to the sidelines, brought back for consultation, maybe reborn into another document, and eventually end up in the trash or permanent storage. The process is very circular and records may go through the loop many times before meeting their end.

Active Use
The Birth of a Record

Records are born into an organization by arriving from the outside or being created internally. Forms management, reports management, and correspondence management help to keep the costs of records creation reasonable. Records management planning that starts at birth can reduce handling costs, and increase control during the entire life of the record. Standard ways of identifying forms and correspondence can be built in. For example, accounts receivable invoices may receive a bar code label with a unique identifier in the mail room. The bar code can then be used to track the document through its life cycle.

Distribution and Reproduction

Just as information originates both from within and without, it travels in and around the organization and, when needed , back out again – leaving a record trail behind it. Information is rarely created or received initially by the person who needs it. Whether the sharing of information is by networked computers, electronic mail (E-mail), couriers, a central mail room, or combination of these, it is important that it be distributed to the people who need it, in a form they can use, within the time constraints of related tasks. This is often a bottleneck in the information system. If more than one person needs the information, it may be necessary to copy or convert it to another form. Routing errors or workloads can cause delays. Some recordkeeping systems use this opportunity to gain control of records early in the life cycle. It is also an opportunity for excess – making just-in-case copies; generating computer reports no one reads; using the word processor to make a routine letter a work of art.

Use and/or Processing

Most records are used to initiate action or record results. Some are processed quickly and easily. Others may require multiple steps by a number of people. Many records are delayed or lost during the processing stage.

Review and Approval

Most records go through a review and acceptance procedure. It may be short and simple – proofreading a data entry screen, or a complex formal process – choosing between bidders for a large project. This is the stage of life when draft information can become, upon authentication, a document. However, the draft and the document may both continue to exist. Since their purposes are different, so is their treatment.

Referrals, Abstractions, and Complication

If stored records were never used again, we would not keep them. Many times records are pulled out of storage and reused. They may simply be referred to as a record of a previous transaction or the information may be reused. Often information is abstracted or compiled, and another record created. In this stage, draft and relational information can be very important.

Active Storage

Once records have gotten through the intensive handling stages, they are usually stored somewhere that is relatively accessible. This may be an on-line computer or optical disk system, a central fileroom, or a box in your office. The storage allows the record to be accessed with relative ease and speed. The record is not in current use, but may be needed quickly. This is often the point where records are pulled into a formal recordkeeping system, and possibly converted to another medium.

Long Term Storage

At some point a record's information is either not needed or very rarely referred to. For a memo on holiday hours, this may be shortly after its creation, while a set of building plans may be kept on hand for decades. The primary requirements at this stage of life are the ability to destroy records on schedule, to preserve the remainder in usable condition until time to be destroyed, and to be able to locate them on the rare occasions they are needed. Low-cost storage is usually a higher priority than speedy access. Records are generally sent to long term storage for one good reason — a planned transfer to less expensive storage — and several bad ones: the active records storage area was too full; someone left records in their office and their replacement did not know what to do with them; or "just in case." Sometimes this is the first time a records manager has control of the records. It is also the point at which many records are converted to another medium. This is often the caretaker stage.

Death and Destruction

Only a small percentage of records are immortal. The rest should be destroyed. The use of high density storage media encourages us to forget to destroy records. When a box of microfilm can replace a storeroom full of paper, the pressure to destroy records to make room for others is reduced. People are reluctant to discard old diskettes. They agree, "It doesn't take up much room and one of these days I might need it." While it is true that the problem is smaller, being literally miniaturized, it is not gone. Eventually even miniature records cause storage problems. But more importantly when you save unneeded records, fewer resources are available to manage the records you really do need.

Table 14: Management Concerns and Needs by Stage of Life and Functional/ Structural Combination

Relational Information				
Relational information comes in small pieces that are linked to provide information. The information can be rearranged as needs dictate. Often relational information is extracted from documents and relates directly to supporting documentation. *Audit trails* may be extremely important to show how data is manipulated. There is often a desire for more relational information but *capacity* and *creation* costs are often high.				
	All Structures	**Unit**	**Transaction**	**Reference**
Use	Speed of access. Creation control and cost. Accuracy.	Avoid fragmentation of information.	Ability and ease of extracting, compiling, and calculating with selected information is often a key concern.	Least often backed by or created from documentation Maybe a third party database.
Active Storage	Pulled in and out frequently. Maintain integrity. Speed of access. Ease of access.	Decision to update or replace information. Deletion or correction.	Purge by date. Length of time on-line directly related to volume and system capacity.	Replacing information more common than purges. Eliminating information no longer needed and not replaced can be a problem.
Inactive Storage	Short term. Primary reason for storage is backup.	Usually not kept.	Audit trail.	Discard.

Putting It All Together

In combination, the purpose of the record, its structure, and its stage in the life cycle create some management needs. The following charts describe baseline needs and concerns, regardless of circumstance. How important these needs are and the priority to the organization are determined by organizational considerations, which we will discuss in Section 7.

Publication	
Primary goal is accurate, current information in a uniform format available to many. The original copy is kept by the publisher, but it is classified and treated as a document.	
	Reference
Active Use	Cost of creation, ease of access, and distribution are key concerns. More resources are expended to make information accessible as frequency of access and importance of accuracy increase.
Active Storage	If not handy—it often will not be used. If not used, do not store. Screen records replaced regularly, discard outdated material. No long-term storage for publications.

Draft	
Primary purpose should be a guide or boilerplate to create new letter, report, spreadsheet, etc. Decreases keystrokes and increases accuracy and consistency. In practice, may be substituted for document, a poor practice.	
	Reference
Active Use	Easy to find. Compatible with software packages. Easy to use.
Active Storage	Access is vital. Protection against damage or loss. Capacity can become a concern. Purging is usually a document-by-document decision. Should not be sent to off-site storage.

Documentation			
Reliability is key as this is the type of record that is most often called into court and accepted to substantiate testimony.			
	All Structures	**Unit**	**Transaction**
Use	Control cost of creation. Often received from outside so controlling and incorporating into system are key. Authentication ability.	Avoid fragmentation. Keep unitized information together.	As volume or importance of transaction increase, so does need for speed and control.
Active Storage	Volume and capacity problems. Cost of space has to be weighted against need for proximity.	Good maintenance required. Ways to determine that files are closed. Decide how long closed files are kept before transfer.	Cross-indexing may be needed to pull together a "case" for transactions with a common theme.
Inactive Storage	Proximity less of a concern. Retrieval more of a problem as volume increases and personal knowledge of where to find information decreases. Accuracy of refiles important.	Date of closure is important for retention.	Often need cross-references.

Section 4: Variations and Permutations of Media

Section 2 discussed the physical aspects of each medium. This section is a brief discussion of some of the ways each medium can be utilized. This is not meant to be a definitive study of all the possible alternatives. The purpose is to show that each medium has many possible applications.

Paper Handling Alternatives

Most people are familiar with the ubiquitous four-drawer vertical file cabinet. It is not the only place to store paper. Many types of shelving are available, offering from 20% (five-drawer cabinet) to over 300% (high-density mobile shelving) increases in filing capacity in the same space. The use of color-coding schemes can decrease retrieval times and reduce misfiles. Centralizing files and enforcing a good checkout system help to control losses and misfiles. Barcoding makes it possible to track records either on a document or a folder level. Computers can be used for indexing, tracking, and locating paper records. The cost savings from alternative media often come from reducing the cost and time required for retrievals along with increased control over the records. Space savings alone will rarely justify the cost of a change in medium.

Micrographics

While all microfilm is essentially comprised of reduced photographs of paper, there are variations. Most of the variations focus on matching the layout of the film to the structure of the records and to the access system.

Roll microfilm has thousands of images on one roll. Prior to the development of computer-assisted retrieval, images on the film had to be arranged in a logical sequence so they could be located when needed. Newspapers arranged by date and page number are an application commonly seen in libraries. Roll film is also used for files in inactive storage. Since all the records for a given period are complete, they can be filmed as filed. Personnel folders can be arranged in alphabetical order and filmed. Invoices can be arranged by date and vendor and filmed. Files of this nature are often arranged so that access can be direct. The arrangement mirrors the structure of paper records. Computer-assisted retrieval has made it possible to film more randomly. Documents can be filmed immediately after processing, rather than waiting for a complete file folder to be created. The index, rather than the arrangement, points to the location of the record. Even when individual records are randomly filmed, there should be some logic to what is on each roll.

Microfiche was developed primarily to fulfill the need for unitized records. A smaller number of records are stored on each piece of fiche (typically, 98 images for filmed documents and 208 for COM (computer output microfilm), so filming can be done more quickly. One does not have to wait until several thousand images are collected before filming the documents. With roll film, the original paper record is often sent on a regular basis and then replaced with a microfilm copy at the end of the month or year. With fiche, copies can be produced and sent quickly enough to completely replace the paper copy. This is especially useful for periodic reports and publications where each set of records is complete.

Unitized records — such as personnel, contract, project, etc. – are also suited to fiche. An individual's personnel file can be one set of fiche, rather than part of a roll with other people's records. Unitized records can be produced after a record is closed or while it is still active. Updating microfiche is done by film jackets or by specialized camera/film combinations. To produce jacket fiche, film is shot on a roll and then cut into strips and inserted into transparent sleeves. Then copies are made onto microfiche. As information is added or changed, film can be removed from the master jacket and new copies made to replace the old. Some methods of updating microfilm involve films and cameras that allow the addition of images to the original film.

Microfiche are often harder to control than microfilm, because it is easier to lose or misfile a single fiche than an entire roll of film. Good titling, color-coding, and notches to show the position in the file can help avoid these problems. Automated retrieval systems for microfiche are available, but tend to be expensive. They are not as common. The cartridges hold a number of fiche and the camera is able to move directly to the desired image. But because they must move in three dimensions (up and down through the stack, then to a given row and column), the design is more complex and less standard than the design for automated retrieval of roll film. Often the arrangement of microfiche is very similar to that of paper file folders. The primary differences between microfiche and paper files, in this type of system, are that microfiche offers: decreased size, increased document integrity, and fast, inexpensive copies.

Aperture cards are a form of unitized film holding a single image per unit (it is possible to have several smaller images of each card, but this is rare). Maps and drawings are the most common application. Any application where an individual image is a complete record, needs to be tracked individually, and is over-sized may be suited to aperture cards. Aperture cards have space for eye-readable information and can be punched with encoded information to allow rapid sorting and retrieval.

Microfilm is generally produced in one of two ways: directly as computer output, or filmed from paper documents Computer Output Microfilm (COM) can be printed on-line or off-line from data on tape. The ability to print off-line makes the use of service bureaus or consolidated COM services practical in many cases. COM basically replaces, or supplements, computer-printed data. Most COM output is character-based, although graphic COM is available. COM output can be either roll or fiche.

Source record cameras vary greatly in price and features. The two most common types of cameras are planetary and rotary. When using a planetary camera the document is placed on a platform (copyboard) beneath the camera. The head of the camera can be moved up and down to adjust the reduction ratio. Rotary cameras take the document into an enclosed body and pass the document in front of the camera. The reduction ratio is fixed by the camera head used. Changing reduction ratios means changing the camera head. Both types of cameras can adjust the lighting to compensate for differences in documents. Higher priced cameras automatically sense changes in color and contrast on the original and adjust for it. Rotary cameras cannot handle rapid changes from original to original as well as planetary cameras. Primarily due to the high filming speeds, there is not enough time to react and readjust where there are rapid changes from record to record. The amount of adjustment for size is also more limited, due to the high speed, the fixed maximum width, and the fixed reduction ratio.

Rotary cameras usually have an automatic or semi-automatic feed. Some can also duplex documents (film both sides in a single pass). Rotary cameras are generally much faster than planetary cameras. However, because of the automated document handling and the limitations on depth of focus, rotary cameras are best suited for documents that are uniform in size and quality. Checks, for example, are rarely filmed on anything except a rotary camera. Rotary cameras have a fixed maximum width for originals, but the length may be indefinite. Continuous forms or long documents, such as geographic logs, are well suited for filming on rotary

cameras. Planetary cameras are often hand-fed—an operator places each page on the filming surface and takes a picture; removes or flips the page; and places and films the next page. Some newer planetary cameras have automated document handling – much like that of copy machines. Planetary cameras often give the best results when the record quality is mixed, the sizes are mixed, and/or the originals are fragile. Planetary cameras are also the only way to film bound volumes without dismantling them. Very large documents are filmed on planetary cameras designed to handle the size and lighting requirements for maps and drawings.

Step-and-repeat cameras are basically planetary cameras that capture images directly onto microfiche. Some versions use dry silver, to allow for instant processing, or updatable film technology, allowing for very rapid updating of microfiche files. The tradeoff is that the film is not archival quality and is subject to image degradation and loss with time, use, and exposure to the environment.

Cameras can also make locating images easier. Most cameras are capable of marking the film in some way. The most common marking is a blip. There are three sizes of blips that can be made. They are used primarily for retrieval from roll film. A reader/printer with a specialized controller counts the blips of a given size or sizes and moves to the desired location. With single blipping, every frame may be marked or the beginning of each record (which may be any number of pages). Dual and tri-level blipping allow for a hierarchical access to records. A well-designed scheme of blipping older records may preclude the need for an index. For example, old contracts could be filmed in numerical order. Each contract has several multi-page sections, but they are in a consistent predictable order. A tri-level blipping scheme will help users find the section needed in less time than it takes to pull paper records, without indexing. Rolls are marked with the range of contract numbers. A large blip separates each contract. A medium blip separates each document and a small blip separates each section. The controller allows the searcher to speed through the film by blip size or frame by frame.

Frames may also have a sequential frame number marked on it. Other readers use an odometer to measure the image's distance from the beginning of the roll. The odometer reading is stored as the location. Other encoding schemes have been used, such as barcoding the location, but most have been dropped in favor of the blipping system. Blips also

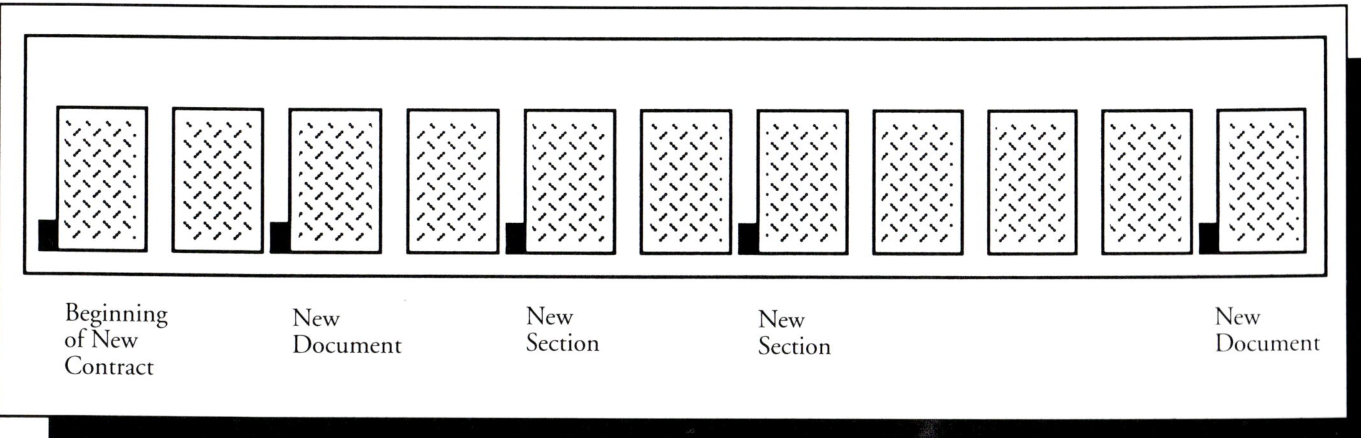

Figure 7: Example of Tri-level Blipping Scheme

assist in positioning the film automatically. Printing, as well as retrievals, can be done quickly.

Some cameras and reader/printers help automate indexing. They interface with a computer and can automatically record the roll and frame number while accepting data input specific to the record. Some cameras are capable of scanning and reading a bar code on the record as it is filmed. A computer stores the barcoded indentifier along with the roll and frame location.

Cameras are being developed that will not only film images but scan and digitize them as well. This will allow the simultaneous storage of records on film and as electronic images.

Microfilm images are examined with either a single-purpose viewer or a reader/printer. Very sophisticated reader/printers are available. Zoom lenses can adjust for variations in reduction ratios without changing lenses. They can also zoom in on a selected portion of the image to make it more readable. Many reader/printers come with a computer assisted retrieval system that automatically locates images on a given roll. Printing can be done page-by-page or the reader/printer can be programmed to duplicate a given set of images. Some new reader/printers scan microfilm images from the film. A digitized image rather than an enlarged photo is the result. The digitized image may be printed on a laser printer or faxed to another location. These reader/printers are very new: improvements and changes are being made rapidly.

Several companies have plans to make reader/printers that will allow the digitized image to be transmitted via a network to an individual's workstation.

Magnetic Media

All information regarding magnetic media is not necessarily a records management concern. Many of the details of how the machines actually produce the desired effects are best left to trained specialists. Where data processing and records management meet is the *management* of information, deciding priorities and allocation of assets. Records managers also become concerned with magnetic media when: the information and medium are retained beyond active use; the record may need to be used to substantiate decisions; the information is used to manage records; and/or the data is used to create new records. Again, the focus is not on the technical methodology, but the management implications for speed, reliability, costs, control, etc.

Very rarely will a records manager be directly involved with the magnetic media in a central computer facility, except possibly with tape storage. Most organizations require that backup tapes be stored off-site in a controlled environment. The concern of records managers is generally focused on the provision of suitable storage, timely and accurate retrieval, and preservation of the tapes.

Records managers tend to be more involved with magnetic records produced by personal computers and word processors. This is because the information is generated at the user level with few of the controls imposed by a centralized computer facility. Users will often substitute or supplement hard copy information with computer data. It is not unusual for users to file magnetic disks in with paper records or box up disks and send them to the same storage facility used for paper. Magnetic tapes must be taken out of storage periodically for retensioning. They also need to be examined for data loss on a regular basis, as random data loss can occur for no particular reason.

One challenge is to assure that magnetic media are used appropriately and not kept beyond their useful life. The other challenge is locating specific data files. Naming conventions, identification of removeable media, and systematic storage practices are needed with magnetic media just as with any other record.

Optical Disk

Optical disk offers four distinct variations of media: Compact Disk-Read Only Memory (CD-ROM), Write Once Read Many (WORM) disk, rewriteable disk, and WORM tape) and three distinct applications: publications, image storage, and storage of machine-readable information.

Publications
CD-ROM

CD-ROM is a publishing medium. The practicality of using CD-ROM for publishing depends on how various factors interact.

The first step in producing a CD-ROM is to acquire the data in machine-usable format. This is often the most complex and expensive step in producing a CD-ROM. The information may be in the form of images, encoded information, or both.

Next, the data is edited and organized into a consistent format. Then the information is "authored." Authoring is the process of combining the data, adding codes, defining blocks of data, identifying references, compressing images, and making other format changes to optimize the data for CD-ROM format. Authoring software is designed to format the information for use with matching retrieval software. The retrieval software determines how the user will access and view the data. After authoring, an index is built to speed retrieval. The information is then premastered: formatted on tape. The tape is usually sent to a service bureau that produces a master. A heavy metal plate is formed from the master. The metal plate is used to stamp the information into soft plastic which is coated with aluminum and then with a protective covering.

A single CD-ROM holds 550 megabytes, about 137,500 pages of paper (close to a ton in weight), the equivalent of 382 1.4 megabyte floppies, or about 12,000 images (8.5" by 11" at 200 dpi (dots per inch) with a compression factor of 10). It would take nine days to transmit the data on one CD-ROM via a 2400 baud modem. CD-ROM is being used to replace many printed publications, to distribute databases, and to provide machine-usable copies of forms, clip art, photographs, maps, etc.

Most of the expense associated with CD-ROM mastering is in the collecting, preparing, and indexing of data. The cost depends on the type of data and how it is to be retrieved. Standard retrieval software can keep the costs down, if it is suited to the application. Stand-alone PC workstations are available that can handle the tasks of authoring, indexing, and downloading to a tape for mastering. In high volumes, CD-ROM can cost as little as $2.00 each. At low volumes, one company offers mastering plus one hundred copies for about $5,300. So cost ranges between $2 and $53 per copy. The price is low enough that the decision to use a CD-ROM should be driven by factors such as the cost of preparing the information, the number of copies needed, the value of document integrity, the volume of the information, the frequency and urgency of updates, and the installed base of hardware.

<h2 style="text-align:center">Table 15: Variables in Choosing CD-ROM as a Publishing Medium</h2>

Cost to Collect and Prepare Data	Most of the cost is for converting data into machine-readable format, authored, and indexed.
Value of Information Integrity	Information cannot be inadvertently changed, yet it can be accessed easily and repeatedly. As the value of the information integrity increases, the benefits of using CD-ROM as a publishing medium also increase.
Volume of Information	Practical for as little as 20 megabytes of information and can hold the equivalent of six encyclopedias. While low volume does not preclude the use of CD-ROM, other variables will drive the media decision. If the volume is large, this may be the overriding reason to use CD-ROM.
Frequency of Updates	Updates can be issued frequently, even weekly, if the information base is large enough, the changes are significant enough, and more than 100 copies are issued. Since most of the expense involved is the initial preparation of data, good procedures can speed the update process and keep costs reasonable.
Installed Base of Hardware	Using CD-ROM requires specialized hardware. The target audience must have the hardware or have it supplied as part of the conversion to CD-ROM.

Part of the price for using CD-ROM technology is exacted in the careful data preparation, good indexing, specialized retrieval software, and hardware needed. But since standards and procedures have been established, the experience base for CD-ROM publications is large and growing. The rigid requirements also make good management of records an inherent part of using the medium.

WORMS and Rewriteable Disks

WORMS and rewriteable disks can also be used as a publishing medium. They are not as well suited for publishing as CD-ROMs for the following reasons:

- Each must be copied individually rather then pressed. This can be very time-consuming.

- Media costs are much more expensive – about $250 per disk.

- The formats, drives, and software are not standard.

The best publishing applications for WORM and erasable disks are those that involve distributing very small databases. Updates can be issued via magnetic disk or modem and downloaded onto the optical disk.

Storage of Images

Using optical disk technology for imaging melds several developments. It combines high density information storage, scanning, compression and decompression algorithms, improved data transmission speeds, computer graphics, increased processing speeds, and the development of better databases. Without all the pieces coming together, optical disk technology would not be viable.

Media & Disk Access

Both WORM and rewriteable disks are suitable for storage of images. Concern is often expressed about using rewriteable disks in a system where maintaining document integrity and validity is important.

Manufacturers have responded by making rewriteable disks that are either write once or write many, but not both. This attribute is built in at the factory and cannot be changed. The advantage to using two versions of the same medium is that rewriteable disks are expected to be demanded in greater volumes than write-once disks. This will help bring the cost of the media down. The choice of disk technology should follow the choice of hardware, software, and standards – not vice versa. The primary concern for records managers is the proposal for standards that mix write-only and rewriteable on the same disk. While this may be ideal for mixing images that won't change with an index that will, it may shake management confidence in a medium that will already be viewed as somewhat experimental and risky. If this type of disk is used, testing and procedures must be extremely careful and well documented, should the accuracy of the data ever be called into question.

Table 16: Criteria for Choosing between 12-Inch and 5.25-Inch Optical Disks

12-Inch Disks	5.25-Inch Disks
Advantages to using this size increase with: – Data volume. – Number of users. – More random storage and access. – Data on-line longer. – Larger data files.	Advantages to using this size increase with: – Fewer requests. – More volatile data. – More utilized data. – Less random access. – Frequent distribution of changes.

There are some standards for drives for rewriteable and WORM disks, however, many manufacturers prefer their own specifications. Alternate designs may allow for faster access or the use of more than one type of disk. Since the industry is young, the struggle for domination of standards continues. This makes sharing optical disks with other systems more of a problem. Several companies have disk drives that will read CD-ROM as well as write to WORM or rewriteable disks. This can help to compensate for some of the compatibility problems. Disks also come in a variety of sizes, causing further problems with compatibility.

There is no particular advantage to any size. The larger disks hold more data, but the smaller sizes spin faster. Usually the choice is between 12-inch and 5.25-inch optical disks. Some very large systems use 14-inch platters which generally hold disks over 12-inches. Table 16 gives criteria for choosing a size.

One disk will not hold enough images to satisfy the requirements of most imaging systems for long. Jukeboxes have been developed for 14-inch, 12-inch, and 5.25-inch disks. Most jukeboxes are designed to use 12-inch disks. The jukeboxes hold a number of platters and one or more disk drives (usually a minimum of two to allow for copying, as well as faster access). Jukeboxes can be joined to increase the capacity of the system. The access time for a system with a jukebox is slower than for a single disk system because the jukebox must mechanically locate the correct disk, slide it into the drive, bring the rotation up to the correct speed, and *then* access the correct spot on the disk. However, jukeboxes vastly increase on-line capacity. The average access time can be reduced by adding drives and using magnetic buffers. With a buffer, images are read onto magnetic media and kept there while demand is active. Because the same document is often called for several times during the workday, the buffer keeps a more accessible magnetic copy at the ready.

Another way to decrease access speed and to keep the size (and cost) of the jukebox minimal is to carefully plan how information will be written to disk. If the retrieval rate of the record is directly linked to the age, then strictly sequential recording makes sense. If the record is usually retrieved along with related documents, then it may make sense to write all related records for a given period to the same disk. For example, if contract compliance records are being kept, and a total of five disks are needed to store all the records for a year, each disk could store records on contractors with a specific range of names or numbers. While the storage density on an individual disk might not be maximized, the access times would be decreased. Additionally, disks are taken out of the jukebox after a certain period to make room for new data. When an old disk is needed, it is inserted manually. If the information in the example above was arranged randomly, all five disks might need to be brought back in order to retrieve all the information on one contractor versus just one disk if arranged by contractor.

Scanning

Images are digitized by a scanner and stored on optical disks. From the user's point-of-view, there is little difference between the working of a flatbed scanner and an office copier. The resolution and contrast can be controlled within certain ranges. Most have resolutions between 100 and 400 dpi. There are some camera-based scanners which substitute a light sensitive photoconductor for film. These scanners move under the direction of a computer and have resolutions ranging from 200 to 2000 dpi. They are generally more flexible and more expensive than flatbed scanners.

Raster scanning is a relatively simple work process. However, because everything on the image is digitized, not only does the image suffer from specks of dust and lint, but a price is paid in terms of storage. A speck of dust is large enough to add about 10 bytes to a compressed image. A dark line on the left side of a page that is only 1/20 of an inch wide will add nearly 3000 bytes to the compressed image when scanned.

Scanners are currently being sold that will scan images from microfilm onto optical disk. Most of these systems are new. One concern in scanning film and transforming it into an electronic image is the degradation in image resolution. If the original film is in poor shape, a 200-dpi copy may not be very legible. Other reasons for the limited number of installations is that most organizations do not need to convert old microfilm records to a medium whose primary advantage over microfilm is increased access speed. Most records that have been on microfilm for any period of time have a fairly low access rate.

Transmitting Images

There are stand alone systems where one operator both scans and retrieves images. Copies are printed out and sent to the requestor. However, most optical disk systems operate via a network. Optical disk images must be transmitted electronically from the controller to requesting workstations. The cable type and the transmission speed affect how quickly documents are transferred. Higher compression factors speed transmission times. Sending images via modem is possible, but unless special communication systems are in place between locations, transmission speeds effectively reduce such transmissions to occasional rather than routine usage.

Displaying and Printing Images

Users of optical disk imaging systems may view images on their workstation if it is linked to the network that has the optical disk storage system. If not, records can be printed and sent to the requestor. High resolution, graphics monitors are required to display images on screen. Newer personal computers generally have the graphics capability, but may need some modification for use as an image retrieval workstation. A special board for decompression of images is often needed. Extra Random Access Memory (RAM) may be needed, especially for multi-page documents. Because there are no input/output delays when using RAM, there should be enough RAM to store all the pages in an average size document. If not, flipping through the pages is delayed as the image must be retrieved from disk storage. Most people are willing to wait a few seconds to receive a document, but not to turn pages.

Many systems utilize PCs or other workstations that are upgraded to allow access to a network, the mainframe, and the imaging system, while still running their own programs. This avoids the need for multiple workstations on one desk.

Processor

Images are large data files, so moving, manipulating, and displaying them takes a lot of computer power. A control unit or server is needed to manage the optical disk system. The controller handles both filing and retrieval of images. As images are scanned they are usually written to magnetic disk first: checked, indexed, and then written to optical disk. The controller usually holds the indexing information. Images are pulled off optical disk and written to magnetic media for quick access and sent to the requestor. Usually the workstation is smart and has sufficient RAM to hold the full document in RAM plus redraw and refresh graphics quickly. CPUs range from a powerful personal computer, through dedicated mini-computers, up to mainframes. A PC performs well for a stand-alone. Because the capability and capacity of PCs have increased, more PCs are being used to run OD applications that are plugged into an existing network. Mini-computers are generally used in networked, turn-key systems. Minis usually have more potential to add RAM and disk space. However, the lines between the PC and the mini are blurring quickly. Mainframes can also be used to manage an optical disk system. The advantage is that most users are already linked to the mainframe. The disadvantage is that the intensive CPU activity required to manage images may degrade overall mainframe performance. Many mainframe terminals are dumb, they have no processing capability. These terminals generally cannot handle images and if they do, this degrades overall performance as the demands on the central CPU increase. When a mainframe is used for an imaging application, plans must allow for growth to handle the increased demands.

Limitations and Opportunities

Optical disk applications, especially networked applications, offer the quickest access of any of the media. They allow many people to share the same images. However, access is limited to people who are tied into the system. Routing and long-distance movement of images is still too difficult and costly for most organizations. Either a great deal of transmission time or very high speed communication is needed. Additionally, the cost of using optical disk includes the equipment and software required to manage, file, and access records. The cost of management overhead increases with optical disk. An optical disk system still necessitates good records management and it adds the additional burden of equipment and software management.

Storage of Machine-Readable Data

Optical disks are not limited to storage of image data. In fact, applications designed to store machine-readable files are growing rapidly. Optical disk is not replacing magnetic media; access is too slow for applications requiring intensive disk reads and writes. It is, however, being used for applications where the advantage of massive storage outweighs the disadvantages of slower access.

The role of optical media for machine-readable information storage is primarily archival (taken off-line and stored). It is used as a backup medium. Even write-once media are useful in this role. The capacity is so great that successive genera-

tions of backup can be kept, which is often an advantage. At this point, disks are most widely used. New tapes are available that will hold over one terabyte on a single tape. Because optical tape is more stable and requires less upkeep than magnetic tape, the use of optical tape is likely to grow rapidly as standards are established.

Another use of optical disk is printing computer output. Sometimes referred to as COLD, Computer Output Laser Disk, the process is similar to producing COM. Reports are written to the disk rather than, or in addition to, paper. In most cases, the print file is dumped to a tape and then downloaded to a PC or minicomputer that extracts index data and writes the report to optical disk. Reports can then be viewed on-screen or printed on a laser printer. Since information is stored, not images, the capacity is very high. A one-gigabyte disk can hold the equivalent of 250 million printed pages (over 1.5 tons of paper). Forms overlays can be used so the reports appear just as they do printed onto original forms, checks, invoices, etc. The advantage over COM is that the index can point not only to a specific report, but a specific place in the report. When searching an account ledger the index can be designed so that a specific line in the report can be accessed directly. This, of course, greatly reduces searching and access time as compared to COM.

The only limitation is in the equipment. Microfiche viewers are very inexpensive and widely available. To use COLD reports, hard copy printouts must be made or the users tied into a system that can pass the information to their workstations. However, COLD can be tied into most mainframes. The information is character-based, the amount of data passed is small, and no graphics capability is needed, so COLD can be very accessible.

The Role and Place of Fax Machines and Electronic Mail

Fax machines and electronic mail (E-mail) are technologies that offer enhanced communications, and some headaches for records managers if not properly managed. There are very real advantages to the increased speed of communications and exchange of ideas using E-mail and fax transmission.

Fax machines most often print directly onto paper. When important transactions are based on fax transmissions, many experts advise that commitments should be followed-up with an original, signed document. Legally (see the quote below), a fax transmission can be considered a copy in some cases.

Admissibility of reproduced records in evidence.

If any business, institution, member of a profession or calling, or any department or agency of government, in the regular course of business or activity has kept recorded any memorandum, writing, entry, print, representation, or combination thereof, of any act, transaction, occurrence, or event, and in the regular course of business has caused any or all of the same to be recorded, copied, or reproduced by any photographic, photostatic, microfilm, micro-card, miniature photographic, or other process which accurately reproduces or forms a durable medium for so reproducing the original, the original may be destroyed in the regular course of business unless its preservation is required by law. Such reproduction, when satisfactorily identified, is as admissible as the original itself in any judicial or administrative proceeding whether the original is in existence or not and an enlargement or facsimile of such reproduction is likewise admissible in evidence if the original reproduction is in existence and available for inspection under the direction of the court. The introduction of a reproduced record, enlargement, or facsimile does not preclude admission of the original. This subsection shall not be construed to exclude from evidence any document or copy thereof which is otherwise admissible under the rules of evidence. 28 USC 1732, Judiciary and Judicial Procedure 115-Evidence; Documentary.

The primary problem is that some fax copies do not have a high enough resolution to be considered an accurate reproduction and many of the papers used for fax copies are not durable.

The use of computer-based faxing also means that copies of faxes can both be printed out and stored on disk. Until the fax is printed out it is not on a durable medium and its acceptability is dubious.

E-mail allows people to exchange notes electronically. It is widely available and useful for communication within the same building, across the country, or across the world. Internal E-mail may be passed through a mainframe and/or network. Remote access is through modems. E-mail is easy to use when traveling to stay in touch with the office. E-mail also helps avoid the problems of telephone tag.

E-mail is both character and image-capable, so the information in a note can be extracted and put into another document.

E-mail notes may be stored by individuals and/or the system, generally on magnetic media. It can also, like any file, be printed.

Facsimile and E-mail are very attractive, and popular, communication options. However, the very advantage of easy access and informal, ad-hoc communications can cause records management headaches. Often the information in these communications is not as private as assumed. The general lack of structure and audit trails leaves the information in a shady area, from a legal standpoint — especially if needed to prove a point in favor of the organization. However, the same information could likely be used against the organization. The presumption is that you are not likely to fabricate unfavorable information, but may be tempted to be creative in modifying or creating records to show you and your actions in a favorable light. Users need to be made aware of these pitfalls in using these methods of communication. Some guidelines are:

- Include in the communication only information and opinions that would not embarrass you if made public.

- Purge old E-mail and fax copies frequently and regularly.

- Have a procedure for making permanent, accurate copies, and authenticating them when the information may be needed for evidentiary purposes.

Section 5: Finding Records

Better and more efficient records storage is worthless if you cannot find records when you need them. Methods of finding records range from locating them quickly with the aid of a powerful database to the dreaded "stop and drop" (where everyone stops what they are doing to search frantically for a missing record.) Our ability to store information far exceeds our ability to organize and retrieve it efficiently.

A discussion of finding records can be confused by semantics, so we need to define a common vocabulary.

- **Location.** This is where the record physically resides:
  The fileroom, 4th cabinet, 2nd shelf, 12th file, 3rd document back
  Track 48, sector 12
  Box 132 on aisle 6, shelf 3, folder 2
  Roll 139, frame 1007

  Knowing the exact physical location varies in importance. Sometimes identifying the primary container is sufficient. For magnetic and optical systems the user may need to know the container, but only the software is concerned with exact physical location.

- **Arrangement.** How containers and records are physically ordered.

- **Container.** The physical element of storage that holds the record. There may be layers of storage: a file in a drawer in a cabinet; a piece of fiche in a given drawer; a specific disk in a jukebox; etc.

- **Index.** A reference that points to the location of a file.

- **Classification.** Group of records related by common function, structure, retention, and handling requirements.

- **Indentifier.** A specific characteristic of a record. A unique indentifier is linked to one individual record.

Finding information is a challenge regardless of the medium. As direct access becomes more limited, the need for, and accuracy of, methods to find the right record become more important. In an emergency, paper and film files can be directly accessed and searched. Direct access to magnetic and optical media is theoretically possible, but it is the equivalent of searching through a dumpster filled with one-and—a-half tons of randomly arranged pages. Theoretically possible: not feasible. Therefore, the need for better access planning increases as records move to media that are less directly readable by the human eye and as the density of records (number of records per given amount of space) increases.

Arrangement

Physical arrangement can be the system for finding paper and film records. It is an important element in most systems. Physical access can be random, direct, or hierarchical.

- Random arrangement means the record location is placed in any open location. This is often acceptable or even desireable when dealing with the smallest storage unit — a magnetic or optical disk or even a file folder. For example, flipping through thirty or forty pieces of paper when a file is pulled requires less effort than trying to keep all papers in all the files arranged in a specific order.

- Direct access means a unique identifier allows the user to go directly to the desired records. For example, pulling Joe Doe's emergency notification card from a file arranged in order by name is a simple task.

- Hierarchical arrangement groups records by common identifiers and subcategories. For example, grouping may be by class, then date, and then by a combination of one or more identifiers. Each grouping is arranged in alpha, numeric, geographic, subject, or some other order. There may be several levels of organization. Figure 8 illustrates a sample hierarchical structure for a set of purchasing files.

A well-designed hierarchical arrangement can aid greatly in finding files. For many systems, it is the only method needed to locate files. Some hierarchy in arrangement may be needed regardless of media. For example, separate optical disks may be used for records from "A" to "M" and those from "N" to "Z." The exact arrangement of records within the container depends upon the volume of the records, the indexing system (if any), and the needs of the organization. Totally random arrangement is rarely efficient. At a minimum, there should be an arrangement scheme for containers.

Figure 8: Hierarchical Arrangement

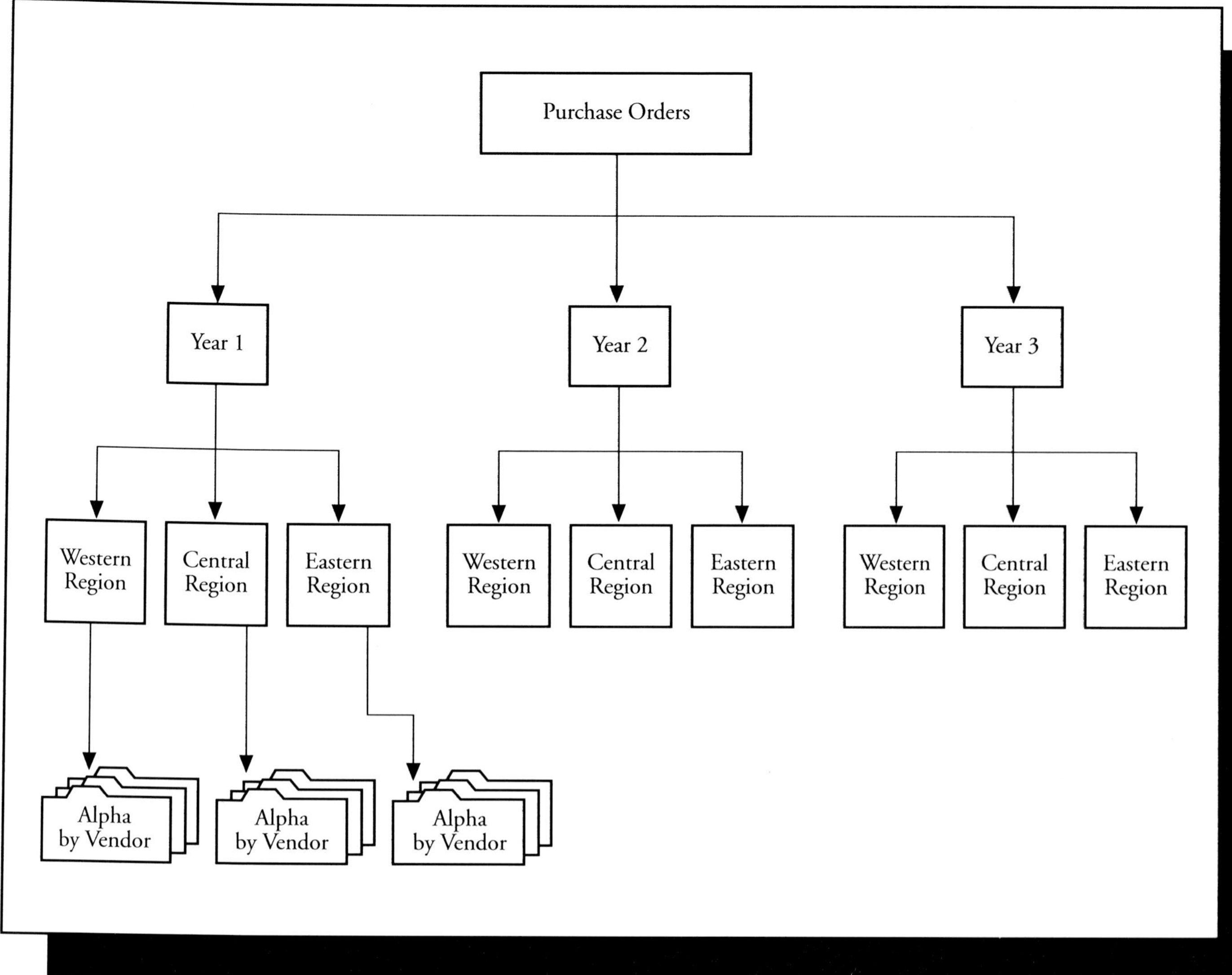

Classification

Regardless of their arrangement or any other method of access, all records need to be organized into functional groupings. The system may be very simple or rather elaborate. Classification is a logical grouping of records by common factors which requires that all records in the group have the same retention period. Indexing and arrangement schemes do not have to be the same for different classes. Nor does the medium need to be the same for each.

A good classification system can be the basis for integrating all the different recordkeeping systems within an organization. A good classification system provides the overall framework for identifying the characteristics, uses, retention, quantity, function, and value of each set of records. This type of grouping is also refered to as a record series. The procedures and tools for handling each group can be appropriate, yet quite different.

Indexes

Indexes are an indirect method of finding records. You use index information to find the records you need when the arrangement of the records is not sufficient for locating them directly. Using the example in Figure 8, if a purchase order from January, Year 3 from the Acme Vending Company on a item purchased by the Western Region is needed, the user does not need an index. The hierarchical arrangement works well when the year, region, and vendor are known. But if all purchase orders for items over $100,000 are needed, the only alternative to an index is a search of all the records. An index allows more flexibility in finding records. Physical arrangement imposes a given structure and relationship between records. Indexing allows a logical change in the relationships as information needs dictate.

Indexing can dramatically improve paper and microfilm systems. It is an inherent part of magnetic systems: the purpose of some of them. It is a critical factor for the success of optical imaging systems.

Indexes are not a panacea. They take time to design, time to create, time to maintain, and storage space. As the index grows in size and flexibility, it also tends to grow in complexity. The costs of data input, storage requirements, and search time must be balanced against information needs.

An ideal index allows users to ask for information in their own words. The indexing system helps them quickly refine and target their request to find exactly the right records. This type of index is not possible with today's technology. Choices have to be made. Simple indexes are usually the easiest to build and maintain. They are also the least flexible. More complex indexes offer more flexibility, but require more expertise in building, maintaining, and using them. The most successful searchers are aware of the limitations, structure, and vocabulary of the index.

One key to success in indexing is consistency. A consistent vocabulary needs to be agreed upon. Identifiers should also be consistent. For example, the name of vendors should be entered according to standard rules. Rules for abbreviations must be agreed to. If the index is computerized, thought must be given to how the system will sort entries. When sorting and searching for matches, consistent vocabulary is essential. The computer will treat W. J. Carter and Associates differently than W. J. Carter & Assoc. The same identifiers must be used for each record in the class. Identifying some records by social security number and others by employee badge number complicates searches.

Another key to success is to focus on the needs of the searchers. Build the index upon the identifiers they know and the information they want to retrieve. The design should focus on the most common, most complicated, most time-consuming, and most critical searches. More flexibility usually means more complexity. Indexes cannot be designed to respond with pinpoint accuracy to every possible request. The resources invested in finding the records should be proportionate to their value.

Indexes can point to differing levels. They may point to a box of folders, a particular roll of film, a file folder, a multi-page record, a specific page, or an exact location on the page. The level of the index should be appropriate for the medium and the type of retrieval.

Indexes require considerable time and energy to plan, build, and maintain. Information has to be entered into indexes and it has to be kept current — if a location changes, index information must change. Section Six discusses ways of capturing information for both indexing and storage. Manual indexing is possible for some systems, but not for high volume, high density systems. As the costs of databases have declined and their power has increased, they have become increasingly popular tools for managing and locating records.

Electronic Databases

Electronic databases are becoming an increasingly important tool for indexing records. Databases are integral parts of Computer Assisted Retrieval (CAR) and optical disk imaging systems. Many commercial warehouses use databases to index and track records. More and more media-independent records management databases are being designed. Regardless of medium, a database can be a valuable piece of technology for managing records.

Conceptually, databases are nothing new to records managers. They are simply automated recordkeeping systems. New files are added, new data is put in existing files, data is retrieved from existing files, data is updated, data is deleted, and files are removed. The advantages of having a computer to manage records are: compactness, speed, reduced drudgery, and currency of information. Databases are designed to reduce redundancy, avoid inconsistencies, share data, enforce standards, apply security restrictions, and maintain information integrity. The advantage of databases is that defined rules can be enforced more consistently. For example, when clerks type identifiers on labels, they may forget to indicate the date of creation or may type a 6-digit instead of 7-digit contract number. A database data entry form can require that certain fields (pieces of information) be completed and check the information against a list of rules or specifications for accuracy.

The database consists both of entities, the objects represented by the database, and the relationships that link those entities. The ability to have multiple links and ones that are not necessarily limited to hierarchical relationships, give database indexes the flexibility to provide information in ways that are not possible with manual indexes.

Most databases are created using a standard database package that is tailored for the specific use. Records management indexes need to be designed to:

- Provide the output needed, on-screen, on paper, or to a computer file that can be used by another program.

- Allow ease and accuracy of intensive data entry.

- Increase speed in searching and presenting the number of hits (database records that meet the search criteria) found.

- Allow the needed flexibility for searches.

Database Output

Deciding what information the database needs to provide is an important part of choosing a database and configuring it for use. The most essential output is a list of records that meet search criteria and their locations if needed plus, in the case of some CAR and most optical disk systems, issuing the order to another machine to pull the desired record. Other output can include usage information, management reports, location and tracking of paper records, etc.

Searching Speed

The architecture of a database affects searching speed. How the searching is handled can also impact on the speed of data entry. Searches of a database are very similar to searches for paper files (only much, much faster). Key fields are ones that are indexed. One method of storing files for very quick retrieval is hashing them. Hashed files must have a unique key. The unique key is hashed, that is, an algorithm is applied that assigns a location based on the value of the key. Retrieval is often very, fast. The disadvantages are that the location is tied to the key. The key must be unique. Changing the key also means moving the record to a new location. Accurate data entry of the key is crucial. Storage capacities must be planned very carefully. The amount of space required and the amount actually used depends on how evenly the data is distributed. If the unique identifiers come in predictable, even ranges, space usage is fairly good. Only the searches on the primary key are sped up. Sorts are not easy.

Another index, called a sparse index, stores keys paired with the physical address of the record. To retrieve information a search is made of the index. This type of index allows for both sorting and searching. This index is often the most efficient when the number of records being searched is small. However, searches are limited to keyed fields. As more fields are keyed, more disk space is required for indexes.

B-Trees use a data structure that essentially indexes indexes. Both keyed fields and secondary unkeyed fields can be searched. B-Trees support flexible, complex search requests more effectively than the other structures.

Neither of these structures is inherently better than the others. They may even be used in combination. However, it is important to be aware of the price. If a vendor promises that records will be located in a very short period of time with no

Table 17: Sample Search Requests

Information Needed	Field or Key	Operator	Value	Condition
Find invoice 1234	Invoice number	Equal	1234	
Find all invoices over $1,000 dollars from March	Invoice amount	Equal to or greater than	$1,000	AND
	Date	Greater than	29 February	AND
		Less than	1 April	
Find all employees with medical insurance who do not have dependents or who work for Department X.	Medical Insurance	Equal	Yes	AND
	Dependents	Equal	O	OR
	Department	Equal	X	
Find all contracts for widgets where the total cost is over $1,000,000 but the contractor is not from Butte, Montana	Contract Type	Equal	Widget	AND
	Total Cost	Greater than	$1,000,000	AND NOT
	Location	Equal	Butte, Montana	

degradation as the size of the database increases, realize that this probably means the files are hashed. This speedy access is limited only to requests that ask for the record by the unique key. Keyed fields can speed up requests, but they also require more disk space. It is very possible for indexes to be several times larger than the database. Adding keys also slows data entry. As a record is entered, the index must be updated for each keyed field.

Flexibility of Searches

The flexibility of searches depends on the database structure, the indexing schema (as discussed above), and the query language supported by the database. Search requests are composed of defining what field (or fields) you want to search by; specifying an operator and a value; and possibly adding conditions. The table above lists some sample searches.

Searches can, of course, only be made on information that exists within the database. In some cases, searches may be made only of keyed fields: other fields can be used to display added information in reports, but cannot be searched. All databases allow for finding exact matches. Many also allow searching for ranges of information: greater than or less than. Combined operators — such as *between* (two values), *greater than or equal to; less than or equal to; in* (a list of values) — replace multiple search statements, making complex searches easier. For example, *in* allows requests for records on all employees working in the B, Q, and Z departments to be combined into one, rather than three requests: *Find all employees IN (B, Q, Z)*. Conditions allow one search to meet multiple criteria. Some databases also allow for the use of wild cards when searching. A wild card substitutes for one or more letters. For example, a search for all companies equal to ARM% (% being the wild card for multiple letters) could return ARMENIAN CARPET and ARMY SUPPLY STORE. Wild cards can also substitute for a single letter. For example, a search for invoices matching invoice number 123_56 (_ being the wild card for a single letter) could return 123756, 123956, 123456, or 123056; but not 1234156. Another feature that allows flexibility in matching fields is the embedded string search. This would allow a search that requests all vendors with "FARM" in the name. The possible results could include: FARMER'S NATION-AL BANK, GREEN FARM PRODUCE, and JOE FARM-INGTON'S INDUSTRIES. Another feature is the ability to ignore case sensitivity. This means the requests finds both "MR. Horner" and "Mr. Horner" and "mR. Horner" when requesting "Mr. Horner."

Complex searches take more time. Embedded string search-es, for example, can take a very long time to execute. More powerful searching requires the user to know how to use the search logic. A poorly structured search will take more time to execute and may result in the wrong information. For example, asking for all vendors who are based in Maine or who are based in Washington and are small businesses will result in a list that includes *all* vendors from Maine, not just the small businesses. The search needs to be restated : find all vendors who registered as a small business and (are based in Maine or are based in Washington). A two level interface may be needed: one for the occasional searcher and one for the records management staff.

In any case, the power of the search capabilities needs to match the requirements of the system. The more unique and specific an identifier for a record is, the simpler the index can be, particularly if searchers generally know what the indentifier is. As the database grows larger, the perfor-mance will degrade for searches not done on unique keys.

Text Management and Retrieval

Part of the problem with traditional database indexing sys-tems is that the designer has to anticipate the user's need for information. Generally, the result suffices. Such databases are well suited to large, uniform collections where requests are predictable. However, in situations such as legal and sci-entific research, where search requirements vary from pro-ject to project, an index is much harder to build. As a result, text retrieval methods that offer the ability to search an abstract or the full text of records have been developed. Automated indexing techniques have been developed for this type of task. One method uses a statistical approach that calculates the frequency of each word. The very low-fre-quency, words are removed. Because they appear so infre-quently, it is unlikely they will be used as search terms. The very high frequency words — and, the, if, etc. — are also removed. The remaining medium frequency words are used as index terms. Other times a controlled vocabulary of terms is used. Another method involves interactive indexing where the computer performs the routine indexing tasks and a per-son resolves indexing dilemmas, monitors the process, and edits the results.

Text retrieval works well for systems where records are in machine-readable format, the volume is limited, and flexible access is critical. The drawbacks are: the index can be very large — often larger than the records it points to; the index-ing process requires a great deal of processing time; and searchers need a high level of skill. It takes practice and knowledge of the subject matter in order to construct search inquiries that are both narrow enough to limit the number of hits and comprehensive enough to find the information needed. Effective use of a text retrieval system may require specially trained researchers or at least the availability of expert advice in constructing searches.

Media Considerations

Most methods of finding records are media independent. The reverse is not true: the medium, structure, purpose, and stage of life of the record imposes minimum requirements for finding records.

Table 18: Need to Formalize Methods of Finding Information

	Paper	Microfilm	Magnetic	Optical disk
Media	At a minimum the *container* needs to be identified and *containers* arranged in a logical order. Generally, indexing is by container (file folder or box or both). Rarely are the individual records within a folder indexed.	At a minimum, the *container* needs to be identified and *contents* arranged in a logical order. An index is not an absolute requirement. Both units and individual records are often indexed.	The physical arrangement is important only for machine operations, *an index is required for access.* Magnetic media are often used to create indexes to other records.	The physical arrangement is important only for machine operations, *an index is required for access.* A good index is critical because *each individual record must be identified and indexed.* Very long documents may need indexes to pages within the documents.
	Relational	Documentation	Draft	Publications
Purpose	Indexing is the inherent purpose of most relational systems.	At a minimum, must identify the contents of the *container* and the date retention is based on.	Draft records need a *systematic naming convention.* Use last usage date for systematic purging of draft material.	Related publications, particularly regulations and forms need *systematic identification.* Large publications may require an *index to the contents.*
	Unit	Transactional	Reference	
Structure	Unitized information must be kept together. At a minimum, the *unit must be identified* plus whether it is open or closed. If closed note the date.	A primary identifier is *date of creation.* Generally the *function of the record and a tertiary grouping are also used.*	Reference material is generally identified *by subject matter.*	
	Active Use	Active Storage	Inactive Storage	
Lifecycle	Many records are not identified during their active life. Some control and loss problems stem from the difficulty in locating active records. Difficult to determine if a record exists or was received.	Often the first time a record is identified and brought under records management control. Either the arrangement or an index must point to the records location. The larger the records collection, the more important it is to have an identification system.	The index or arrangement can be the same as for active records. Only with location changes use a new system of locating records. The location system is more critical than for active storage, because of a greater overall volume and less personal knowledge about the records location.	

Section 6: Capturing/Converting Information

Applying technology to records management systems often means transferring information from one medium to another. This transfer can be used either to store a record or to store information about the record. Powerful tools exist to move data from one medium to another. But, as always, no amount of power and technology can replace planning.

Techniques for Capturing and Exchanging Information

The last section illustrated the point that our ability to store information far exceeds our ability to organize and retrieve it efficiently. This section explores some of the technology that allows capturing information to help with the indexing and control of records.

Data Entry/Exchange

Keystroking

Keystroking information is both the most labor-intensive and most common method of recording information on another medium. While many typists are capable of bursts of well over 120 words per minute, this rate is not sustainable. Word processing comes closest to allowing this speed. However, more people are involved with data entry than with word processing. Success in one type of data entry does not necessarily equate to success in the other. We will discuss each type of keystroking separately.

Word processing programs are designed to help speed document creation. They do this by reducing keystrokes and saving keystrokes for reuse. The paradox is that the best typists are often not the most proficient at creating documents. Using macros, glossaries, and style sheets is not intuitive. It takes time and training to develop the ability to use these tools well. A good typist can produce a document much faster if time does not have to be spent setting up a style sheet or creating macros. Learning shortcuts takes an investment in time that pays off only in the future. Well-designed training can help. A program to use experienced word processors to develop standard macros, glossaries, and style sheets can also increase productivity. A good system of file identification and maintenance will also aid retrieval when reusing draft material.

Data entry into a database requires different skills than does word processing. Skilled data entry personnel must often make judgements about *what* to input. Data is entered into short fields in short bursts and then the cursor must be moved to the next field for input. The choppiness of the keystroking does not allow for a high, sustained rate of input. The person doing data entry must also spend time finding the information to enter. Successful indexing requires not just the swift entry of information without error, it requires entering the right information. For example, a person keying information from an invoice may need to find the invoice number assigned by the vendor, the total amount, and the date payment is due. If the information is keyed directly from the invoice, it takes time to find the information. Data input sheets may save time, but time is spent creating them. In most cases, index information for CAR microfilm and optical disk systems is taken either from the original or the image, not from a data input sheet. Unless the index is very simple, data entry people must frequently make judgements about which information is the required information, for example which date to use on an invoice: the date sent, date received, or date paid.

Programs to improve data entry productivity are most successful when they focus on working conditions, procedures, and the reason for errors, rather than simply increasing the number of keys pushed in a given period of time. In fact, focusing on speed frequently increases the error rate. Contributing to errors are: typing ahead of the computer's keyboard buffer, poor layout and design of data entry forms; and poorly designed data entry programs.

OCR

Optical character recognition devices were originally invented in 1912. In 1914, a hand-held OCR device was built as a reading aid for the blind. These early devices had limited

Figure 9: Segment for OCR Identification

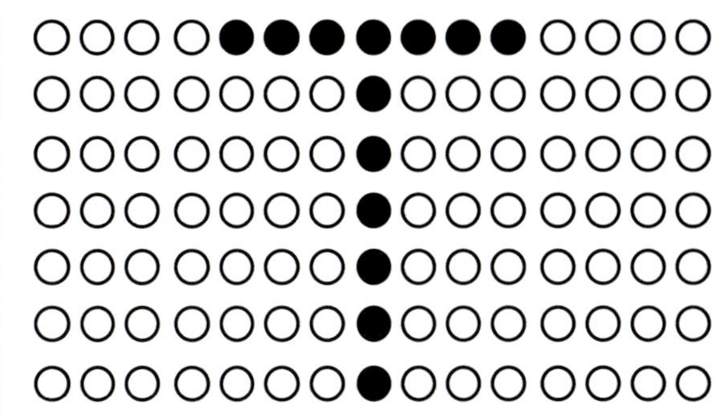

success. For many of the same reasons, their success is still limited.

Scanners work in one of two ways: template (matrix matching) or feature extraction. The page is divided into very small segments and the features examined. To a computer, the letters form a pattern, much like that in Figure 9. With template or matrix matching algorithms, the computer stores patterns that it matches the dot pattern against. It searches through the templates until it finds a match. Then it assigns the computer-code that matches the template. This method of OCR is still crude and slow. Recognition is generally limited to a few fonts. Variations in font size and spacing are not handled well.

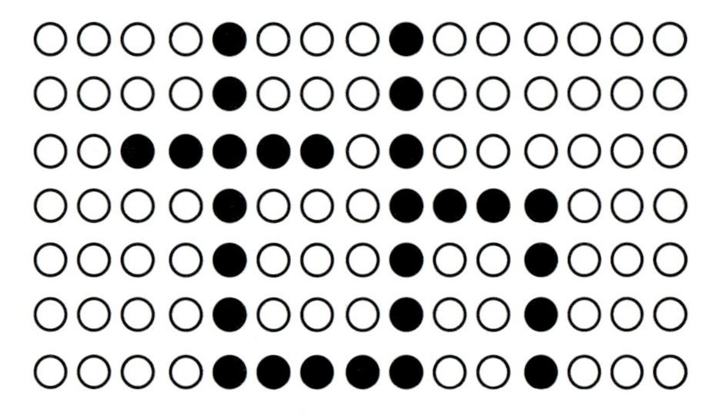

Figure 10: OCR Matrix with Letters Running Together

In text, especially typeset text, where one letter may touch the letter next to it as in Figure 10, matrix recognition software often fails. As the popularity of laser printers and variable space fonts increases, the difficulty of using matrix recognition software is also increasing. This system requires checking each letter against possible templates. Each match is assigned a numeric value representing how well the match fits. If the best fit exceeds a given value, the computer assumes a match has been made. If the best match fails to reach a minimum value, an error character is assigned. Some software uses character frequency rates to speed the process. Matrix matching works well if: the text is typed in a known, mono-spaced, fixed pitch font; the paper is white with a smooth dull surface; there are no extraneous marks on the paper; and the contrast between the paper and the letters is

sharp and clear. Computer memory and processing time limit the number of fonts that can be handled well. Also because the templates are very sensitive to minor changes in the character, a font may not be recognized if the image is skewed for any reason.

In feature extraction, sometimes referred to as topological analysis, the software identifies features in the character images such as the number of loops, lines that cross, descenders, etc. It then uses this information about the pattern to select a character. This type of software can learn new alphabets fairly rapidly. There has also been some success with recognizing printed, handwritten characters. No system is yet capable of recognizing cursive writing, although research and development in the area is intense. The feature extraction process is much the same that we use to recognize letters, but humans are still much better at it than computers. Good OCR software packages are adding more features that mimic human thought in reading. Some of the software uses contextual analysis and spelling checkers to help verify choices. OCR recognition software is probably the most widespread use of expert system or artificial intelligence (AI) software.

In both types of recognition algorithms, speed slows as the dpi resolution, increases, but the number of successful matches generally increases. For low volume OCR users, 60 words per minute is the lowest acceptable rate. For mid-volume users, the rate is 30 to 60 seconds per page (30-60 characters per second), and 1 to 5 seconds per page (400-2000 characters per second) for high volume applications. An accuracy rate of 90% is considered good for OCR. This rate is usually sustainable on good clean type, but may slip to 75 to 80% for dot matrix characters.

Full page scanning works well for capturing text, possibly as part of converting information to be published on CD-ROM. It does not work as well for data input, unless full text retrieval is being used. Wand scanners are often used for data input, many at retail sales outlets. They are generally limited to a small number of characters, use a special font, and either scan only a fixed length or use special start and stop characters. Accuracy on transaction scanners is fairly high. The system works well when there is good control over the records to be input. Forms generated in-house could be printed with a unique number to be scanned in later, for example.

Another application of OCR that has limited but increasing use, is the scanning of a page for conversion to an image and the capture of certain blocks for character recognition. The blocks can be predefined areas of the page or an operator can designate, on-screen, the block to be read. This can afford a slight increase in indexing speed, but due to the error rate and need for editing and review, not a significant increase.

OCR is a field that is fast developing and has tremendous potential — most of it in the future. In the here and now, at least for data input, OCR is of limited value and will not, in most cases, increase indexing speeds appreciably.

Bar Codes

Bar coding has been around since the late 1940's. The first widely used application was developed in 1960 to keep track of railroad cars. Bar codes are widely used in material handling and retail applications.

A bar coding system consists of four elements: the symbol, the scanner, the reader, and the electronic communication. The scanner and reader may be combined or connected by cable. The bar code symbol is simply a set of light and dark bars of varying widths. The width of lines and the pattern they make, represents information. One critical aspect is the width of the smallest element, because that determines how precise the scanner and reader must be. There are hundreds of barcoding schemes, but only about ten are in common use. They are all in the public domain, standardized, and bi-directional (able to be scanned from the left or right, right-side-up or up-side-down) Code 39, or 3 of 9, is the standard format of the Federal Government for markings by contractors. Each character is represented by a group of five bars and four spaces. Of the nine elements for each character, three are wide. (Hence the name 3 of 9 or 39). The complete character set has a stop-start code (interpreted as an asterisk) and 43 data characters. The data characters include 10 digits, 26 letters, a space, and 6 symbols (- , $ / % .). The codes are of variable length. Stop codes indicate the end of code. The code is flexible and relative widths are available over a wide range. Codes can be read by contact wands, hand-held laser scanners, and fixed laser scanners. The codes are discrete, meaning the width of the white space between characters is not part of the code, so their width is not important. It also means the code is bi-directional. The standard density for Code 39 is 9.4 characters per inch. The best first-pass read rate can be expected when the wide-to-narrow ratio of the bars is 3 to 1.

There are two types of errors which occur when reading bar codes, short read and substitution. The use of stop codes helps reduce the short read errors. Bar codes have a relatively low error rate — about one substitution error per 3 million characters. The most common error is a short read, requiring a rescan. When scanning is done by hand, it is fairly simple to simply rescan the code. Microfilm cameras are now available that scan and interpret bar codes as documents are filmed. For these cameras, the placement of bar codes is critical. The bar code needs to be uniformly dark; it must be placed on the page where it will pass under the scanner; and if a high speed is to be maintained, the alignment of the marking to the page needs to be consistent. Preprinting bar codes onto the documents allows the fastest throughput. However, labels with bar codes can be applied to documents and read as well. Bar codes may also be printed by dot matrix and laser printers at the time of origin. The primary problem with this method is ensuring the uniform darkness of the label.

Bar codes work well if the system is carefully planned to incorporate them. They are not the answer to all indexing problems. A unique identifier that is 16 characters or less will work best. If this identifier alone is not sufficient to identify the record, it must be related to data that is already in the database or can be downloaded from another source. An index to records rarely consists of only one field. Therefore, bar codes are most useful when a unique identifier can be placed on a document that links it to an existing database with all the required information.

Bar codes require even, dark printing. If forms are printed in duplicate, scanning the original will give the best results. Documents from an outside source will most likely not conform to your bar code requirements so bar codes must be applied. This can be done in one of two ways. The number can be assigned randomly and a preprinted label applied. When data input is performed, the unique identifier is read into the system rather than keyboarded. The other alternative is to input the information about the record and have the system print a bar code label upon demand. This does not save very much time in data entry, but it does decrease the chances of misidentifying a document. If the barcoding is done as a step in processing, it can also be used to track a document through processing stages. This can be a very cost-effective application for barcoding.

Figure 11: Comparison of Data Input Time and Number of Errors
When Inputting 50,000 Characters

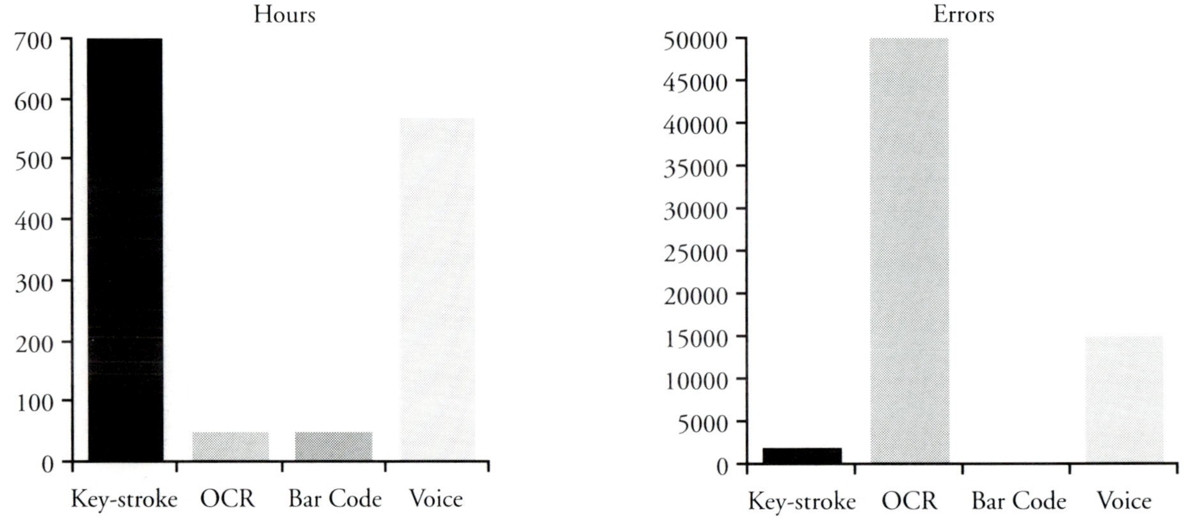

Voice Input

Voice input is an emerging technology that is receiving much attention. Two types of systems are common. In one, the system is trained to recognize the speaker and learns each word individually. These systems can be quite fast and accurate. The other type of system can be used by any number of speakers without training. However, they must speak slowly and enunciate carefully. The speed is much lower and the error rate higher. Of course, as the vocabulary increases (many systems are limited to a few hundred words), storage space and processing time requirements increase. The input rates for speaker-trained systems can approach 500 words per minute with 96-98% accuracy. But they are sensitive to changes in the voice caused by stress or illness. The rate for speaker-independent systems is around 30 words per minute with 75-96% accuracy. At this time, the low accuracy rate, cost, and environmental considerations (primarily noise levels) limit the use of voice for data input.

Data Exchanges

If you have data in electronic form in one system and want to copy it into another, you must to be able to exchange the data. There are several types of limitations. The first is the machine-readable code used. Most personal computers use ASCII, but IBM mainframes use another code, EBCDIC, which means a translator is required. Additionally, many programs add their own unique codes to information. These must be taken out. In order to be used, the program accepting the data must know what information to put into which fields and where one record begins and another ends. Often an exchange of information requires outputting the information from one program in a standard code with standard delimiters and then rearranging the data in the correct order for the next program to accept it. The process of exchange works, but not without some initial effort and planning. The other challenge is working out the communication link between the machines with the databases. It may be a direct link, sharing of diskettes, or tape download. Each machine must be able to read and write a common format. Many standards have been worked out, but all this must be considered in designing a system. The ability to share information easily between databases cannot be taken for granted.

The sharing of information can greatly decrease input time. For example, consider an accounts payable operation. Accounts payable clerks input information on each invoice. Each invoice has a unique number identifying it. When

Table 19: Comparison of Data Entry Methods

Method	Limits		Speed[1]	Accuracy
	Operational	Records		
Key Strokes	Requires training. Data entry is tedious yet requires attention to detail.	Better results if indexed information is in uniform position.	2	1 per 300
OCR	Intensive processing requirements. Large disk space. Very expensive equipment. Requires monitoring and editing.	Clearly defined print. Acceptable typefaces may be limited. Best on white, dull-surfaced paper and black lettering. If indexing, the location of indexable information may need to be fixed.	2-200	1 per 10
Bar Code	Bar code is limited to about 16 characters for most applications. Number must have some meaning or be assigned meaning. Does not reduce number of keystrokes by much but does increase the accuracy and provides for good matching between a document and information already in a database.	Bar codes must be clearly and evenly printed with good contrast. If scanning is automatic the placement of the code can be critical to maintaining input speed.	30	1 per million
Voice Trained for Speaker	Requires expensive equipment customized for the user. Noise can be a problem. Each user must train the system, but since the computer is trained to equate a given sound to a given set of symbols, the foreign language and accent of the speaker are irrelevant. Changes in voice due to stress or illness increases error rate.	Better results if indexed information is in uniform position.	8-42	2-10 per 100
Voice Speaker Independent	Price increases in proportion to flexibility. Very limited vocabulary. Must speak slowly and carefully.	Better results if indexed information is in uniform position.	2.5	4-25 per 100

records personnel index the image of that invoice into a CAR or optical imaging system, they need only record the unique number. The system software records the location automatically. Later a download from the accounts payable system allows the date, vendor number, and amount of each invoice to be added automatically. The downloading and matching are not instantaneous, but can be done unattended.

Image Capture

Images are captured to convert documents from one system to another. Most common are paper-to-film or paper-to-disk, but systems for scanning film-to-disk are being developed and marketed. The primary bottleneck in both filming and scanning paper documents is preparing the documents for filming. Preparation steps include: removing fasteners, smoothing edges, repairing or making photocopies of torn documents, taping very small documents to a larger sheet of paper, and arranging documents in the order they are to be captured.

Filming

Filming can be a very fast method of capturing images. Rotary and automatic feed planetary cameras often have rated speeds of up to 5,000 pages per hour. While automatic stackers are available, they work best on small, uniform documents like checks. Most documents will be hand-fed or stacked in short batches, so the time needed to adjust and feed documents makes 1,500 pages per hour (8.5" x 11" originals) a more sustainable and realistic number. Operators of conventional hand-fed planetary cameras can sustain a filming speed between 500 and 700 pages per hour.

Document resolution remains relatively high compared to scanned images, if the camera is adjusted properly. However, the quality of the image cannot be assessed until an entire roll is filmed and developed. This, combined with the need to group similar documents on a roll of film, means that the turn-around time between image capture and quality control is several hours, at a minimum, and can be several days.

Scanning

Document scanning falls into two basic categories: optical character recognition (OCR) and graphics. OCR translates the image into its component characters and stores it in

machine-readable format. OCR is discussed extensively in the preceding part of this section. For most imaging systems, bit-mapped images are scanned into the system. Section 4 discusses the mechanics of scanning raster (or bit-mapped images). The speed of scanners is usually expressed in the number of seconds required to scan a page. The speed varies from a page per second to almost 20 seconds per page in some low-end systems.

Table 20: Sustainable Scanning and Filming Rates

Sec./Page	Pages/M	Pages/Hr.
Scanners		
3	20	1200
6	10	600
10	6	360
20	3	180
Rotary and Automatic Feed Planetary		
2	25	1500
Conventional Planetary Cameras		
5	12	700
6	10	600
7	8	500

Conversion

When a new medium is chosen for records, the issue of conversion arises. There are two issues to face—what is to be done with the current records and at what point in the life cycle will newly created records be converted.

Converting Existing Collections

Many people approach a change in media as an opportunity to clean up their collection of records and place everything neatly onto one medium. This is usually impractical. More often, some of the records will remain on the original medium. Good reasons to consider conversions are to:

- Keep unitized records together.
- Protect records from environmental damage.
- Preserve vital records.
- Maintain file integrity.
- Prevent loss.
- Make a copy of an entire collection. Sometimes all the records for a particular segment of an organization must be copied — perhaps for a reorganization, a lawsuit, or an investigation. The cost of converting the records may be less than photocopying them.

Converting records to save space is not generally very cost effective. Storing records in a commercial records facility generally costs between \$1 and \$4 per cubic foot. The cost to convert the same number of records involves so many variables that a meaningful dollar figure can not be given.

This discussion will focus on the conversion from paper to film or optical disk. These are the most common and most difficult conversions. Converting records for publication on CD-ROM was discussed in Section 4. Converting machine readable data from one format to another is a technical problem that requires more machine time than people time.

When and What To Convert

Poorly conceived conversions can seriously hamper the success of a new system. The longer the retention period for the records, the more massive the possible conversion. If possible, implement the new system from the start date forward and avoid converting records. This avoids straining the system. Conversions require overloading a system designed for on-going operations, buying excess capacity, or use of a service bureau. Conversions strain management and personnel. Any new system requires training and involves a learning curve. New methods and procedures need to be tested, implemented, and adjusted. If, at the same time, a conversion has to be managed, this adds stress to the people involved.

Possible alternatives to massive in-house conversions are:

- *Use a service bureau to handle the conversion.* This is a particularly good idea if personnel are not yet trained to operate the equipment.

- *Convert as needed.* Convert records when they are requested from storage. This allows conversions to be incorporated into the daily workflow and converts only those records that are actively used. Records not requested before the end of their retention period will not be converted.

- *Do a good-enough conversion.* Many systems require intensive indexing. When converting old records, limit the indexing to just the essential fields. Index the entire record instead of each document. Retrievals will take longer, but older records are likely to be retrieved less often.

- *Convert first.* Use the conversion project to develop workable procedures and get workers trained and proficient. Errors will not be as critical, or as public.

Conversions can be worthwhile, but be sure the added expense and workload are worth the effort. If the conversion is large and essential to the success of the project, planning must be very careful and the cost and time projections realistic.

Estimating Costs and Length of Time

Estimating how much a conversion will cost and how long it will take is a difficult task. Like many projects, a carefully calculated estimate is one that is exceeded only two-fold rather than three times. To make a good estimate the following factors need to be known:

- The size of the record collection. The best way to determine this is to statistically sample the collection. Use a statistical package that gives a range of numbers based on the confidence interval. Give your calculations of cost and time a range based on the estimates of the collection size. You need to know :

- The number of records.

- The number of pages per record.

- The percentage of the records that are double-sided.

- The physical shape of the records. Determine these characteristics while sampling the records. The time required to prep are and film the records increases directly in relation to size, diversity, and the number of records in poor condition.

- The dimensions of the records. Do the dimensions vary?

- The condition of the records. Will repairs be needed? How sharp is the contrast between the image and the background?

- Ranges in the weight of the paper.

- Indexing needs. What information will be included in the index? Is some of it in a database that can be downloaded to the index? How easily can the indexers determine the unique identifier, and other keystroking needs, for the records? If bar coding is to be used for active records, can they be utilized in the conversion?

Collecting this information will provide the basis for determining the number of hours involved in the conversion process. Once the required hours have been determined, the timing of the conversion will depend on the number of people and the amount of equipment allocated to the project.

The first step is document preparation. At a minimum, records must be taken out of storage containers (cabinets or boxes); the staples, paper clips, and other fasteners removed; and sorted into the correct order for filming or scanning. This amount of preparation requires about one hour per thousand pages. Weeding out documents, rearranging them, logging them in, repairing them, or other special requirements add to the preparation time. Preparation time usually requires a minimum of 15% of the total conversion time. The percentage increases rapidly with the amount of preparation required. Preparation is very labor intensive. There are no technical tools to speed the process. It is also an essential step in the success of any conversion. Only careful management attention, good procedures, motivated workers, and good training (all the old fashioned stuff) can increase production in this step of the conversion.

If part of the reason for a conversion is to gain control over poorly maintained records, the conversion will include the cost of repairing long-term neglect. Filing problems often have to be rectified before conversion. Otherwise you will convert trash into expensive, hi-tech trash.

Indexing was discussed in detail in Section 5 and above under data entry. Generally, no time can be saved by using bar codes in a conversion project. If bar codes are used, they must be printed and matched to the document, negating any time savings from reduced keystrokes. Despite the extra time required to bar code, however, the extra control and reduced errors in matching document location and the index could be worth the investment.

The time spent capturing the images is not the most critical. Indexing time almost always exceeds the scanning or filming time. Quite often preparation time also exceeds scanning or filming time. The speed of the equipment chosen can be selected to match either the current workload or the expected capacity of the system. Electronic images are available immediately after scanning. Microfilm has to be processed and quality checks made of the film before it can be used. This time must be taken into consideration when planning a conversion.

Figure 12 shows the number of work hours required to convert 50,000 documents. It also shows graphically the percentage of time spent on each task.

Table 21 shows how many people will be needed to convert 50,000 documents in either one or two weeks. A productive time of seven hours per day is used. This allows for two 15-minute breaks, time to get ready in the morning, and to put tools away in the evening. No allowance is given for supervisory time or time spent doing routine computer maintenance (like backups).

The length of the conversion period, the equipment required, and the number of people needed are directly related. In this example, a one week conversion would require 3 conventional planetary cameras or scanners versus 2 for a two-week conversion. In fact, it seems that a two week conversion schedule that ran a part-time shift, could get by with one camera or scanner. Good information on the size of the collection, the sustainable speed of the equipment, and the organization's priorities are needed. If the employees involved in the project are not experienced, extra time must be incorporated for training and the learning curve.

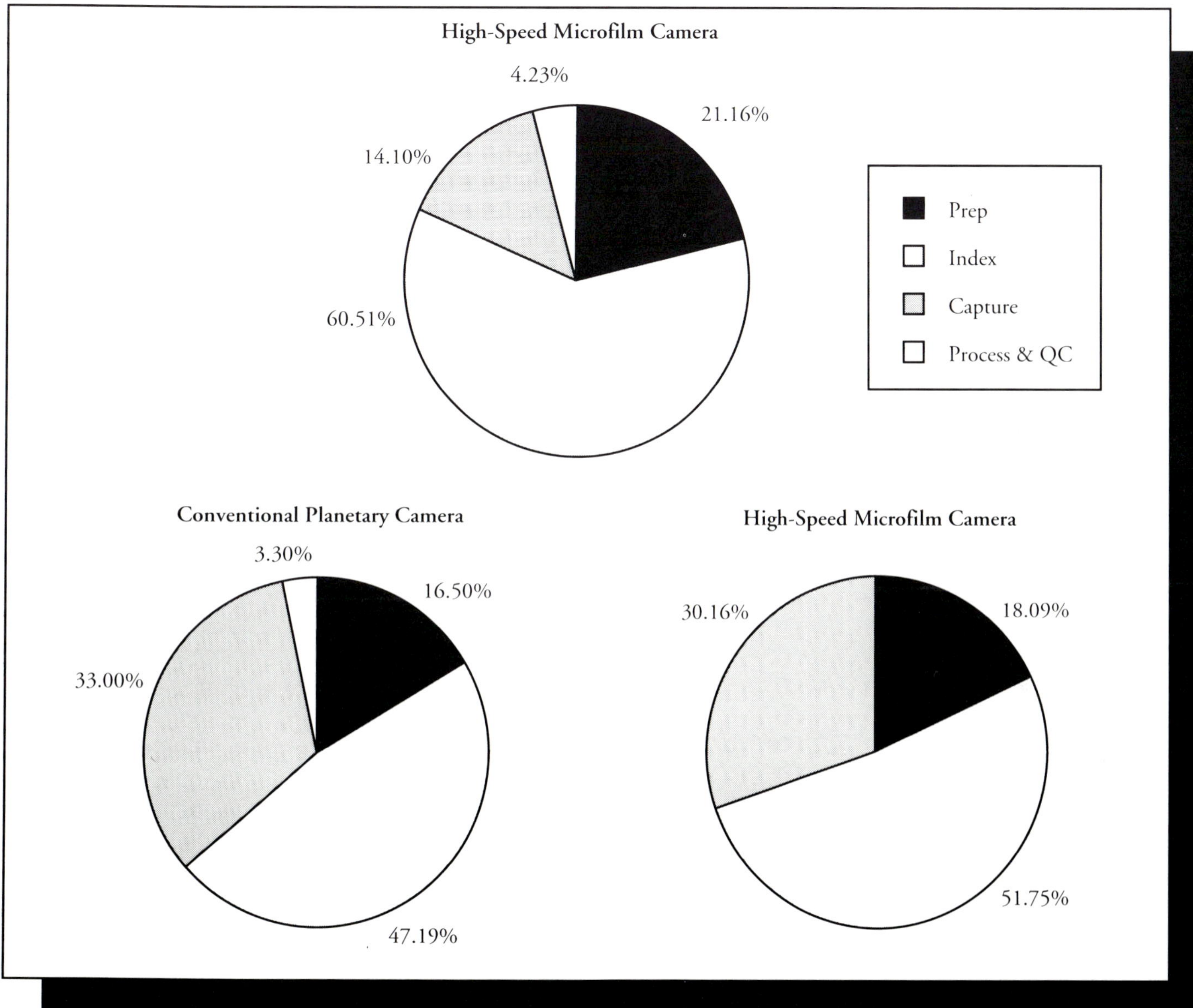
High-Speed Microfilm Camera
4.23%
21.16%
14.10%
60.51%
Prep
Index
Capture
Process & QC
Conventional Planetary Camera
3.30%
16.50%
33.00%
47.19%
High-Speed Microfilm Camera
30.16%
18.09%
51.75%

Table 21: Personnel Required to Convert 50,000 Documents

	One Week			Two Weeks		
	1	2	3	1	2	3
Record Prep	1.4	1.4	1.4	0.7	0.7	0.7
Indexing	4.1	4.1	4.1	2.0	2.0	2.0
Film/Scan	1.0	2.9	2.4	0.5	1.4	1.2
Process & QC	0.3	0.3	0.0	0.1	0.1	0.0
Total	7	9	8	3	4	4

1= High speed rotary or auto-feed planetary camera.

2= Conventional planetary camera.

3= Medium speed scanner.

Service bureaus will usually quote conversion price—generally a given price per thousand documents. The cost will vary according to the overall size of the project, the amount of preparation needed, and the indexing requirements. The advantages to a service bureau are: the cost is fixed; service bureaus generally have the staff and equipment to meet your deadlines; and they train the staff and correct errors at their expense, not yours. However, the agreement must carefully state how records are to be prepared and how indexing information is to be decided. If the requirements are clear and standard, there should be a minimum of problems. If there is much ambiguity, a potential problem exists. Sometimes the best approach is to provide personnel to work with service bureau personnel on document preparation and indexing. In any case, time must be spent controlling what has gone to the service bureau, what has returned, verifying quality, and tracking progress. Even with a service bureau, conversion can require a great deal of time from your staff.

Incorporating Conversions Into Routine Record Handling

More important in the long-run are conversion procedures for new records. Probably the most important decision is when to convert the documents. The most common points are in the mailroom (as they are received), at the file cabinet (active storage), or at the records center (inactive storage).

Converting records as they are received gives the greatest control over them. If the record can be processed on the new medium, the potential for savings and improved service is very high. The problems to resolve are: how will the records be diverted from the normal workflow to be captured; how quickly must the conversion be done to prevent interfering with the workflow; and what is to be done with the original records?

Converting records after processing and before storage also requires a quick turnaround. These records are still highly active and the unavailability due to conversion should be very short. The primary sources of savings from converting at this point are the savings in floor space, the benefits of increased control, and the benefits of increased availability.

Converting records prior to off-site storage presents the fewest problems. The records are not as active so turnaround time is not as crucial. The payoffs from converting at this time are also more modest. The primary benefits are the protection of vital records and maintaining document integrity.

Section 7: Cost Considerations

The question of what a recordkeeping system costs is not an easy one to answer. A simplistic approach to costing is foolish and misleading. The true cost of a system is far more than the amount paid to the vendor. Only by understanding the true costs of records can the opportunities for savings be seen.

The cost of using a medium is an extremely important factor when making choices. However, it is often difficult to calculate the full costs of *any* record system. Beyond the obvious costs of space, labor, and equipment there are also opportunity costs, the value of the information itself, and the value of compressed response time.

Direct Costs

Direct costs are by no means the full costs of a system, but they cannot be ignored. Because records deal with information, we have to go beyond obvious costs to assess the real importance of records. At the same time, we cannot forget the obvious costs. Direct costs must stay in proportion to the benefits.

Space Costs

When calculating space costs it is important to include the square footage occupied by the equipment, access room, aisles, and work area. This is the direct cost for space. Microfilm and optical media can reduce storage space for records up to 95%. However, while the media might *fit* in a broom closet, you will rarely put them there. Space must be allowed for staging and handling records, document preparation, filming/scanning, data entry, and retrieval devices. It is unlikely that space costs will be reduced 95%. However, the advantage of using a higher density medium is that the growth can be accommodated for a longer period of time.

In reviewing opportunity costs, cost avoidance must also be considered. When an organization runs out of records storage space, unless the way records are stored is changed, the costs include the additional space for records *plus* costs for redesigning space and moving. A change that allows an organization to avoid expansion accrues the benefits of *not* paying for expansion.

In some organizations, there is no way to add space. Therefore space savings become a critical element. The choice, then, is not whether to change, but what to change.

Supplies

Determining supply costs for microfilm, magnetic, and optical media is relatively simple. Yet, a common problem is ignoring the cost of supplies when calculating system costs. In some systems, the cost is significant enough to influence the choice of systems.

Determining the full cost of supplies for paper systems is more difficult, primarily because costs are dispersed throughout the system. Rarely are the costs for folders kept separate from the cost of paper clips. Additionally, because the costs for individual supplies in paper systems are relatively insignificant, they are often overlooked. Twenty-five cents for one file folder is insignificant, but the total cost for thousands of folders is significant.

Labor

People expend recordkeeping time in five ways: filing; refiling; searching; getting to the records; and waiting until records are found. Regardless of the medium or system, all these tasks are required. The differences are found in who performs them and how long it takes.

Determining labor costs would be easy if all recordkeeping functions were performed only by specialists. But almost everyone in an organization is involved with records in some way. Even well-organized executives, with dozens of assistants, occasionally look for records and spend some time waiting for someone else to bring them records. The increasing trend toward fewer clerical and support personnel often means managers and other professionals spend a larger percentage of their time in recordkeeping tasks. Saving small amounts of time for a large number of people can be significant in the aggregate. Saving just fifteen minutes per person per day totals to 65 hours in a year, 1300 hours a year for a work group of twenty.

Rarely does changing recordkeeping systems allow an organization to reduce the number of employees. More often the effect is to reduce the overall rate at which employees are added and to increase the amount of work each person can perform. The records management staff can handle more records with the same number of people and the rest of the staff spends less time on records functions, freeing them for other work.

Equipment

The entry costs for some recordkeeping systems, particularly optical disk systems can be very high. More options are becoming available, and affordable. But as it stands now, a well-integrated imaging network with about 20 workstations costs about $1 million for equipment, supplies, software, and technical support. This cost may be much less if the organization already has some of the infrastructure needed to support optical imaging. Additionally, much of the equipment is multi-purpose. It will benefit overall operations, not just records management.

However, the entry cost for special application optical systems is quite reasonable. CD-ROM drives can be purchased for under $500 each. Costs for systems to print computer reports on optical disk, COLD, start around $30,000. They can be easily integrated with the existing infrastructure because the information is character, rather than image, based.

Hardware costs for a high-end microfilm system are about forty percent less than for a optical disk system of the same size. The equipment is specialized. There is rarely any synergy between microfilm and other information applications. However, a well-run microfilming operation can fill the needs of many organizations.

The possibility of doing a better job with paper should not be overlooked, particularly if budgets are tight. Major improvements can be made with a minimal investment. Often, improving the management of paper records can pave the way for a smoother transition to another medium in the future.

Indirect Costs

Everyone acknowledges that better information can increase productivity. However, agreement on what makes information *better* and exactly how it will increase productivity are rarely agreed upon. Part of the disagreement is the difference in goals and priorities. Another is the difficulty of assigning a dollar value to better information.

Value of Information

The value of information was discussed at length in the introduction. All information is not equally valuable and it is not equally valuable at all times. Some of the ways information varies in value are:

- *Time Value.* Information wears out and is replaced. The value declines with age. The rate of decline for a particular record classification or series is fairly predictable.
- *Cost of Loss or Delay.* The value of information is enhanced by having it when and where you need it.
- *Intrinsic Value.* Inherent historical or esthetic value.
- *Vital.* Some records are so important that their loss could severely cripple the organization's ability to perform.

Opportunity

When a new system reduces the time a manager spends waiting for information, we rarely replace the manager, but we do have the *opportunity* to use that time more effectively. While it is difficult to quantify opportunity costs, they exist and wise decisions will take them into account.

Conclusion

It is often hard to quantify the savings of very large complex information systems. Many of the savings tend to have strategic value. When an organization has to rethink how it processes records, it can often make substantial gains in customer satisfaction, reduce time spent in work process, and enhance its ability to react quickly to highly critical information demands.

Looked at very simply, the cost of media rises as information moves from paper to microfilm to magnetic and optical media. However this focuses on capital outlay. Decisions made purely on this basis ignore the purpose and value of information. Costs can be approximated by industry averages, but *worth* is a function of the values and priorities of the organization.

Section 8: Organization Considerations

Until the needs and priorities of the organization are considered, no decisions about a medium's suitability can be made. A series of forms are included to help you assess your organization's operations, records, and resources. Just as all the information in an organization is not equal, neither are all the records. These evaluation forms are designed to be most useful when focusing on records and the element of the organization that uses them. These forms are simply a tool. Like any generic tool that is applied to a specific situation, some modification may be needed.

Using the Analysis Forms

The three sets of evaluation forms focus on operational concerns, records considerations, and organizational resources. A score from -100 to +100 is assigned to each factor that applies. A negative score is given to factors that management wants to avoid. For example, on Form 1, an organization that does not want any transactions to go beyond five days may assign negative scores to factors 7.6 and 7.7. They could then give items 7.1 through 7.5 scores representing the percentage of transactions that should meet those deadlines. Factors that are not applicable should be left blank. There is room to add factors. Figure 13 illustrates how two different organizational components might use the same form.

The scores should reflect management's objectives and willingness to commit resources to achieve those objectives. If all the scores are the same or within a limited range, the forms will not be useful.

These forms are only one method of evaluating priorities. Any process that helps an organization evaluate its specific needs and requirements is valuable.

Operational Concerns

Form 1 concentrates on analyzing operational concerns–how records are used within the organization. The assessment form can be used to assess the organization as it is or as management plans it to be.

Most of this focus is on workflow. In examining workflow, we look at how records *move* through an organization and at their *function* in the organization. Records flow through an office for three reasons: to disseminate information, as part of a work process, and/or to record an activity.

Many records are part of a transactional process: they either stimulate a transaction or are created in response to the stimulus. Accounts payable invoices and claims forms are two examples of records that initiate a transactional process.

In many organizations, the management of records begins at the end of the workflow. One reason for making changes is

Figure 13: Using Analysis Forms

Form 1: Operational Concerns

RECORDS SERIES CLIENT CLAIMS	ORGANIZATIONAL COMPONENT CLAIMS	
MANAGEMENT CONCERN	PRIORITY	NOTES
1. Internal Distribution		
1.1. Speed	30	AFFECTS PROCESSING COSTS & TIME
1.2. Distance	10	
1.3. Reduce delays	30	
1.4. Accuracy of delivery	30	EACH CLERK GETS SPECIFIC CLAIMS
2. Shipping/Mailing		
2.1. Bulk	0	
2.2. Quantity	70	LARGE AMOUNT SENT THERE
2.3. Distance	0	U.S. MAIL FIRST CLASS
2.4. Speed	0	CURRENT SYSTEM WORKS WELL
2.5. Safety	0	
2.6. Reduce delays in handling	0	
3. Electronic Distribution		
3.1. Graphics	65	ENCOURAGE FAX INPUT
3.2. Machine-readable		
3.3. Quantity	15	ONLY 3 FAX MACHINES
3.4. Person-to-person		
3.5. Place-to-place		
3.6. Speed		
4. Portability		
4.1. Used in-house		
4.2. Used by travelers		
5. Conversion Before Processing		
5.1. Turn-around	85	MUST BE FAST
6. Transaction Characteristics		
6.1. Value	75	
6.2. Quantity	100	HUNDREDS PER DAY
7. Transaction Life		
7.1. On-the-spot		
7.2. Under 4 hrs.		
7.3. Same day		
7.4. One - two days	85	GOALS
7.5. Two - five days	10	VERY IMPORTANT!
7.6. Five - ten days	5	
7.7. Over 10 days		

Form 1: Operational Concerns

RECORDS SERIES DIRECTIVES: FORMS /PUBS	ORGANIZATIONAL COMPONENT DIRECTIVES	
MANAGEMENT CONCERN	PRIORITY	NOTES
1. Internal Distribution		
1.1. Speed		
1.2. Distance		
1.3. Reduce delays		
1.4. Accuracy of delivery		
2. Shipping/Mailing		
2.1. Bulk	100	VERY BULKY – CONSTANT
2.2. Quantity	100	SHIPPING LARGE AMT DAILY
2.3. Distance	80	ENTIRE COUNTRY
2.4. Speed	40	
2.5. Safety	85	SPECIAL DISTRIBUTION MGMT
2.6. Reduce delays in handling	25	
3. Electronic Distribution		
3.1. Graphics		
3.2. Machine-readable		
3.3. Quantity		
3.4. Person-to-person		
3.5. Place-to-place		
3.6. Speed		
4. Portability		
4.1. Used in-house		
4.2. Used by travelers	80	USED IN FIELD
5. Conversion Before Processing		
5.1. Turn-around	60	
6. Transaction Characteristics		
6.1. Value	40	INDIVIDUAL VALUE LOW
6.2. Quantity	100	
7. Transaction Life		REFERENCE NOT TRANSACTION
7.1. On-the-spot		
7.2. Under 4 hrs.		
7.3. Same day		
7.4. One - two days		
7.5. Two - five days		
7.6. Five - ten days		
7.7. Over 10 days		

to get control of records earlier. The efficiency of office workers is linked to workflow. The ability to reduce the transaction life of a document offers the organization a way to process more transactions and better serve its clientele. Operations cannot be improved if we do not understand and examine them. We also need to differentiate between the limits imposed by the physical aspects of the media versus the work patterns imposed by tradition — *we do it this way because that's the way we have always done it.*

The evaluation form is linear, but the workflow generally is not. Some steps may be skipped and others repeated several times. The weight given to a factor should reflect both the impact it has on the organization and the need for control.

Form 1: Operational Concerns

RECORDS SERIES	ORGANIZATIONAL COMPONENT	
MANAGEMENT CONCERN	PRIORITY	NOTES
1. Internal Distribution		
1.1. Speed		
1.2. Distance		
1.3. Reduce delays		
1.4. Accuracy of delivery		
2. Shipping/Mailing		
2.1. Bulk		
2.2. Quantity		
2.3. Distance		
2.4. Speed		
2.5. Safety		
2.6. Reduce delays in handling		
3. Electronic Distribution		
3.1. Graphics		
3.2. Machine-readable		
3.3. Quantity		
3.4. Person-to-person		
3.5. Place-to-place		
3.6. Speed		
4. Portability		
4.1. Used in-house		
4.2. Used by travelers		
5. Conversion Before Processing		
5.1. Turn-around		
6. Transaction Characteristics		
6.1. Value		
6.2. Quantity		
7. Transaction Life		
7.1. On-the-spot		
7.2. Under 4 hrs.		
7.3. Same day		
7.4. One - two days		
7.5. Two - five days		
7.6. Five - ten days		
7.7. Over 10 days		

Form 1: Operational Concerns

MANAGEMENT CONCERN	PRIORITY	NOTES
8. No. of People Involved in Processing		
8.1. Very small: 1-2		
8.2. Small: 3-8		
8.3. Medium: 9-64		
8.4. Large: 64 or more		
8.5. Well-defined		
8.6. Unpredictability		
9. Type of Task		
9.1. Well-defined		
9.2. Unpredictable		
9.3. Sequential processing		
9.4. Parallel processing		
10. Access		
10.1. Easy to find directly		
10.2. Good cross-reference		
10.3. Speed		
11. Simultaneous access		
11.1. Number of People		
11.2. Speed		
11.3. Copy Consistency		
11.4. Cost		
12. Access Restrictions		
12.1. Low number of people		
12.2. Degree of confidentiality		
13. Dispersion of Work group		
13.1. Same floor		
13.2. Same building		
13.3. Same complex		
13.4. Remote access needed		
14. Record Ergonomics		
14.1. Multiple records viewed		
14.2. Large record size		
14.3. Working comfort		
14.4. Portability		
15. Processing Safety		
15.1. Resistance to handling		
15.2. Environmental requirements		
15.3. Disaster resistance		

Form 1: Operational Concerns

MANAGEMENT CONCERN	PRIORITY	NOTES
16. Standard Practices		
16.1. Equipment used		
16.2. Identification of information		
16.3. Retrieval processes		
17. Equipment to use records		
17.1. Availability of equipment		
17.2. Speed		
17.3. Cost of equipment		
17.4. Compatibility		
17.5. Integration w. other equipment		
17.6. Reliability of access		
17.7. Skill level needed		
18. Integrity of Information		
18.1. Misfile		
18.2. Loss		
18.3. Degree of fragmentation		
18.4. Ease of refiling		
18.5. Control		
19. Accuracy of Information		
19.1. Low error rate		
19.2. Current		
19.3. Consistent		
19.4. Speed of updates		
20. Use of Information		
20.1. Work group only		
20.2. Departmental		
20.3. Organization wide		
20.4. Shared with customers/clients		
20.5. Public information		
21. Data Input		
21.1. Part of process		
21.2. Relates directly to records		
22. Alteration		
22.1. Need to authenticate		
22.2. Change existing documents		
22.3. Add to existing records		
23. Copies		
23.1. Very small: 2-5		
23.2. Small: 11-49		
23.3. Moderate: 50-100		

Form 1: Operational Concerns

MANAGEMENT CONCERN	PRIORITY	NOTES
23.4. Large: over 100		
23.5. Consistency among copies		
23.6. Low turn-around time		
24. Legal Acceptability		
24.1. Audit Trail		
24.2. Trustworthiness		
24.3. Well-tested		
25. Limited Training Requirements		
25.1. Records management basics		
25.2. Equipment use		
26. Active Storage		
26.1. Equipment cost		
26.2. Space reduction		
26.3. Higher capacity		
26.4. Expansion potential		
26.5. Proximity		
26.6. Length of time		
26.7. Environmental requirements		
26.8. Disaster resistance		
27. Inactive Storage		
27.1. Equipment cost		
27.2. Space reduction		
27.3. Higher capacity		
27.4. Expansion potential		
27.5. Proximity		
27.6. Length of time		
27.7. Environmental requirements		
27.8. Disaster resistance		
28. Other		
28.1.		
28.2.		
28.3.		
28.4.		
28.5.		
28.6.		
28.7.		
28.8.		
28.9.		
28.10.		

Distribution and Movement of Records

Internal distribution impacts how records get to the person who needs them, how fast they get there, and how they get to the next person in the process. A higher score for speed (factor 1.1) reflects the need for quicker delivery. A higher weight for distance (factor 1.2) should reflect longer distances. Delays can be caused by poor addressing, uncertainty as to who is to receive the record next, time spent occupying in/out boxes, etc. The accuracy of delivery is a measure of how important it is that a specific person receive the record in a specific sequence. Higher scores for factors 1.3 and 1.4 reflect a desire to reduce delays and improve the accuracy of delivery.

Shipping and mailing costs are incurred when records must move over long distances. The bulk, quantity, and distance travelled are factors (2.1 to 2.3) determined by operational needs. The speed, safety, and lack of delays are factors (2.4 to 2.6) that can be controlled, to some extent, by management.

Electronic distribution allows the rapid movement of limited numbers of records to locations that have matching equipment. Portability is the measure of how easily records can be picked up and used in another location. Records that are used in conferences and meetings should receive a high score. Records that travelers must be able to take with them and work with outside the organization should also receive a high score. The only aspects of conversion considered, at this point, are the constraints on turn-around time, if conversion is to take place before processing.

Handling paper takes the most time and manpower, because each individual record must be handled. Faster distribution requires more manpower. Records are easily lost or misrouted. Better control requires more manpower. Despite the perils and delays of distribution, most paper gets to the right place in time to accomplish the job. The farther paper travels, the greater the chances of loss and delays. If records are routinely shared or processed, proximity is important. Paper is difficult to control. Keeping track of who has a record is difficult and time-consuming. The drawbacks to shipping paper are: high cost, lack of speed, and loss of control. Paper's advantage is its flexibility — there are a number of methods to move records and it is easy to pick and choose among them depending upon your needs.

Microfilm reduces the handling requirements by physically bundling large numbers of records onto rolls or fiche and clearly marking who will receive the bundle. Distribution time depends on manpower and is usually measured in hours. Microfilm is not usually passed around the office. It is too fragile and easy to loose. Microfilm shipping is less versatile and takes just as long (if not longer than paper), but the cost per given volume of records is lower, due to reduced bulk.

Fax machines allow for electronic distribution of both paper and microfilm. High costs and relatively long transmission times limit faxing to small numbers of important records.

Magnetic and optical media distribution time is measured in seconds. Records are rarely lost. However, the recipient must be tied into the system with compatible software and hardware. Records are passed easily, quickly, and under complete control — *if* the people who need the records are linked into the system. Being linked into the system can substitute for physical proximity. Optical disk images are usually transmitted electronically which is fast, and safe. Due to the low weight and high cost of optical disks, they are usually shipped by courier to reduce the chances of loss or damage. Magnetic media are more fragile than optical, but usually safe with special handling.

Transaction Characteristics

A record generally requires that you do one of four things: read it for the information, perform a task, discard it, or pass it on because it is not relevant to your job. Among the possible tasks to perform are: add information from another source, perform a computation, abstract information, check someone else's work, enter information into a computer, or authorize an action.

Most papers received in the course of day's work look alike. Time has to be allotted to read the records and to assign priorities. If a task is dictated, completing it may require other sources of information such as computer printouts of codes, access to a database with names and addresses, a phone book, or another record— buried somewhere in the stacks of paper on your desk. It may involve completing the record, using it to create a new one, filling in a form, making a copy, or all of the above. The predictability of the tasks, the information needed to complete them, and the number of people involved are important in assessing how technology can be best used.

Factor 6 provides a place to measure the value and quantity of transactions. The scores on value and quantity needs to reflect the organization's priorities.

Factor 7 assesses how long the processing period either does, or should, take. The transaction life is the length of time it takes one record to move through the complete processing cycle. Factor 8 reflects the number of people routinely involved in processing the records. Factors 8.5 and 8.6 measure the predictability of who will be involved in processing the records. Factor 9 defines the type of task. Factors 9.1 and 9.2 are self-explanatory. Sequential processing (9.3) requires that each step in the processing be taken in a specific order. Parallel processing (9.4) means one or more steps could be taken simultaneously, if the medium and system support it. These two factors may be given percentages that reflect how much of the processing must be sequential and how much can be concurrent.

Also important in assessing records are questions of access:

> Who uses the records?

> Who should be restricted from using the information?

> How many people need to use the record during the same period?

> How fast is access needed?

Factors 10.1 through 12.2 address these factors. One problem with paper that is not encountered as often with other media is consistency. With paper, it can be difficult to determine if the copy being used is the most current or even that it is complete.

Another important factor in choosing a medium for some records is the proximity of the people who work with the same information (factors 13.1 to 13.4). Organizations with branch offices may perform some tasks in the branch office and then send the records to a central office for further processing. The choice of a medium can impact how the different offices interact. Paper works well for many organizations, but it is somewhat more difficult than other media to control. Magnetic media work very well for sharing relational information, which may also help to control the other media being used. The movement of information from the field to a central office may offer an opportunity to convert records as they arrive with a minimum of interruption in the work flow. Converting records in the field and transmitting film or optical copies is less common, primarily because of equipment costs and turn-around time. Optical disk has some additional barriers to sharing. Unless an entire disk is filled daily and copies made, physical exchange is also cost and time prohibitive. Transmitting a large number of images electronically is usually cost prohibitive. The limitations on

updating and changing microfilm, combined with the turn-around time for conversion make it a difficult medium to use for most widely dispersed work groups.

Ergonomics should not be overlooked. Ergonomic design applies to the comfort in using records as well as machines. While one rarely thinks of paper as being designed, its form is something that has been refined through the centuries. It is comfortable to read; easy to use, whether a single sheet or several multi-page records; and very portable. Factors 14.1 through 14.4 address these needs. The weights assigned by an organizational component that uses single page records and compares them to database information should be lower than those given by another work group that frequently compares several long, complex documents.

Processing safety (factors 15.1 to 15.3) is the exposure to damage or loss a record faces while in use. During the process of carrying out the task, there are dangers to the record. It can be discarded inadvertently. Papers can be shuffled in with other papers and lost. Records come apart, are left on copy machines, have coffee spilled on them, and lie abandoned in in-boxes. Film can be scratched, microfiche mislaid. Magnetic disks, especially floppies, can fail and lose information. Fortunately, most records survive the process intact, and with their mission accomplished. But there are, inevitably, some losses. The environment, the number of people handling the record, and the record's value determine how much effort should be taken to protect information during processing.

Factors 16.1 to 16.3 measure how repetitive and standard the work process is. Automating predictable processes is easier and has more immediate rewards than trying to do the same for less standard processes.

Factors 17.1 to 17.7 measure the impact of both the equipment available and management's attitude toward the need for special equipment during work processes.

Factors 18.1 to 19.4 concern the information itself: how important is it that the information be complete and accurate.

Factors 20.1 to 20.5 reflect who uses the information and how important it is to the organization to make this information available. For example, publications intended for public distribution would receive a high score for 20.5, while a departmental budget would receive high scores for 20.2 and 20.3.

If data is input as part of the work process (factor 21.1) and it relates directly to the records (21.2), then it may be relatively easy to integrate that information into an index, making microfilm or optical disk more viable alternatives.

Approvals are most often recorded on documents with signatures, stamps, and initials. Paper is the only medium with this capability. For film, magnetic, and optical media, new methods must be developed to record approvals. Otherwise documents on these media must be converted to paper, signed, and reconverted. Since signatures are the traditional method of approval, and therefore easiest to defend in court, most organizations will choose to authenticate paper documents and convert them. Adding or changing records is easy with magnetic and paper records. It is more difficult with optical disk and microfilm. Often a new version of the record is scanned or filmed and the index altered to point to the new version. In neither case is the old copy discarded. The new version is simply added to the file. Some forms of microfiche are designed to be updatable, but the process is generally time-consuming. A record can be deleted physically from a roll of film by cutting it away. This is generally not done. It can raise questions of validity and physically weaken the roll of film. Factors 22.1 to 22.3 measure the need to make changes to records during processing.

Factors 23.1 to 23.6 evaluate the number of copies needed, the need for consistency, and the need to make copies quickly. Documents need to be duplicated for two reasons: to share or to protect information. In most cases, backup copies of microfilm and optical disk documents are made routinely. Paper can also be used for backup. However, this is generally not a part of the recordkeeping routine. More often, copies are made by individuals who do not trust the system. In the rare instances where paper backup copies are part of the routine, vital records are usually the only ones copied. It is expensive and difficult to keep copies of paper records (especially active records) complete and accurate.

Legal acceptability varies in importance from one set of records to another. Oftentimes while a record may meet the strict requirements for legal acceptability, it may not meet the traditional expectations of those who will evaluate the record's trustworthiness. Factors 24.1 to 24.3 measure how important it is that the transaction leave an audit trail, is trustworthy, and is *well-tested* in legal situations.

Factors 25.1 and 25.2 measure how much training is required to use the records. Some records systems involve training in records management to use, such as records filed by terminal digits or indexes requiring specialized searching techniques. Other records systems necessitate some knowledge of equipment — operating a power file, a microfilm viewer, or a computer. A higher score indicates management desires *less* training.

After a document has been processed, it is usually stored in a convenient location. The term active storage is used because the newest documents are the ones referred to most often. In general, ninety percent of referrals are made within two months of creation. Factors 26.1 to 26.6 measure the need to keep equipment costs down, reduce space, increase capacity, have room for expansion, keep records close to the users, and increase the amount of time the records are available. Factors 26.7 and 26.8 measure how resistant to the environment and disaster the records need to be, given both the value of the records and the hazards to which they are exposed. For example, a record of moderate value stored and used in a motor pool may have the same score as a more valuable record kept in a vault because of the increased environmental risks.

The number of record referrals decreases rapidly as a document ages. Ninety-nine percent of referrals are made to documents less than 24 months old. The elements in factors 27.1 to 27.8 are the same as for active storage, but reflect the change of priorities for inactive storage. The following requirements, in particular, are affected:

- *Storage Capacity.* Depending on the age of the organization and its retention requirements, the number of inactive records could easily exceed those in active use by five times or more.

- *Security and Environment.* Records need to be protected against loss and damage.

- *Retention Time.* An important consideration is: will the medium last for the full retention period? The answer depends both on the physical characteristics of the medium and the care with which it is handled.

- *Retrieval Time.* There will still be some referral activity. Retrieval time is a function of not only where the records are kept, but the accuracy and completeness of location information as well.

Operating Differences Between Media

Paper is the most flexible medium for processing records. It is comfortable to work with. Part of that comfort may be due to tradition, but part of it is also ergonomic. Paper records are well-designed for human use. Paper is easy to read. Marginal notes can be added, important items circled or highlighted, and changes made. It is easy to compare several documents. Paper is portable. Work can be done at home, on the plane, in the hotel at night, or in a conference room. Information on paper is easy to share. Copies can be made for co-workers, clients, or people attending a meeting. No special equipment is needed to read information on paper. The information can be added and changed easily. Most importantly, paper documents are easy to authenticate. Paper's primary drawback is the difficulty in controlling the amount of time needed for processing. It is difficult to tell whether delays are due to individual work habits or to other factors. Additionally, total or partial document loss is always a danger.

Microfilm use is limited for processing records. It cannot be altered easily. When microfilm is used in processing, it is usually to hold reference information. Microfilm documents rarely initiate tasks, primarily because the turn-around time required between filming and producing usable film is too long.

The role of magnetic records in processing is generally as reference or relational data. Often, part of the processing routine is to transfer input information from other records into a database. The role of magnetic media is generally an adjunct to other media.

Optical disk systems have some work processing limitations. Access to specialized equipment and software is required. Long documents can be very difficult to work with. Depending on the software, it may be not be possible to skip to given pages within a document. Even when it is possible, browsing through an optical disk document consumes the time needed to write the image on the screen. So, comparing long documents is difficult and time-consuming. Because optical disk documents cannot be written on, changes have to be made in a separate step.

The basic advantage optical disk offers in processing work is that the electronic images can be viewed and shared by anyone linked to the system. The remaining processing advantages are a function of software. Some systems will not offer processing assistance. Those that do are usually customized

applications. Part of the difference between optical disk systems is the ease with which programs can be customized or changed.

The processing assistance offered by some optical disk software packages is very powerful. Many systems allow documents to be bundled into packages. Most workstations allow the user to view several documents, and sometimes a computer database, simultaneously. The capability to view several images is called windowing. Using these capabilities, all the information needed to process an invoice, for example, could be sent together. When the user opens the electronic package with an invoice for processing, it may also include the purchase order the invoice is based on, a window to the database with vendor information, and shipping documents. With all the information necessary to make the needed decisions bundled, processing time is cut. Many systems also facilitate document creation through integrated word processing and/or electronic forms. If the purchase order, shipping documents, and invoice do not agree, the worker can call up a window with a standard form letter, fill in the blanks, and have it printed. If there are no problems the worker can fill in part of a forms screen and pass it, electronically, to the next person in the process. After the other steps are complete, the form can be printed, signed, digitized, and passed back to the system. Because electronic forms are often linked to computer databases, information can be pulled from the database onto the form and transferred from the form to the database. This type of link speeds data entry and accuracy, as well as document creation.

Optical disk processing is well suited to systems where:

- A limited number of people process large numbers of documents with common, routine processing needs.

- Simultaneous access to the same document is needed.

- Processing time is critical and needs to be carefully monitored.

- Loss and delay are very costly.

Records Considerations

The second evaluation form focuses on the records themselves. Form 2 starts with the creation of records and goes through their indexing requirements. The weights on this form, except as discussed below, reflect the physical characteristics and uses of the records, rather than management's priorities. For factors where the record meets only one of a given set of criteria, the weight, or impact, is 100. For example, only one retention period (4.1 to 4.8) applies. The applicable period receives a weight of 100. For factors such as 6.1 to 6.7, where a certain percentage of records may meet a given criterion, the weight reflects that percentage. For example, a set of records that is primarily (87%) one-sided, will assign a weight of 87 to 6.1 and 13 to 6.2.

Factors 1.1 to 1.8 concern forms that are created in-house. Factors 1.2 to 1.6 may reflect current conditions or management wishes. If the organization initiates the record, 1.7 is given a weight of 100. If the record is created in reaction to an outside stimulus, such as a check paid on a claim, then 1.8 is given a weight of 100. The factors on conversion (factors 2.1 to 2.4) *must* be weighted. If management will not consider converting records there is no need for this evaluation. Factor 2.1 should be given a score that reflects how fast turn around time needs to be. Factor 2.2 and 2.3 reflect when management prefers to convert records. If a great deal of preparation is needed to prepare the records for filming or scanning, a high score should be given to 2.4.

Factors 11.1 to 11.3 indicate how much control over the records is desired at different points. A high score equates to a high degree of control. Traditionally, records have not been well controlled until filed — active storage. The cost for controlling records during processing can be high.

Factors 14.1 to 14.7 concern how management wants to index records. If records are physically arranged by identifier, an index is not necessarily required. A review of Section 5, *Finding Records,* may be helpful in assigning weights for this section.

Form 2: Records Considerations

RECORDS SERIES	ORGANIZATIONAL COMPONENT	
RECORD KEEPING FACTOR	IMPACT	Weight
1. Record Creation		
1.1. Skill required		
1.2. Equipment cost		
1.3. Equipment availability		
1.4. Turn around time		
1.5. Accuracy		
1.6. Reusability of old copy		
1.7. Initiated by organization		
1.8. Reaction		
2. Conversion		
2.1. Turn around		
2.2. Before processing		
2.3. After processing		
2.4. Preparation required		
3. Type of Record		
3.1. Unitized		
3.2. Transactional		
3.3. Reference		
4. Retention Period		
4.1. Keep under 6 mon.		
4.2. Keep 6 mon. - 2 yrs.		
4.3. Keep 2-5 yrs.		
4.4. Keep 6-10 yrs.		
4.5. Keep 11-20 yrs.		
4.6. Keep 21-50 yrs.		
4.7. Keep 51-100 yrs.		
4.8. Keep over 100 yrs.		
5. Size		
5.1. Uniform		
5.2. Mixed		
5.3. Legal size or less		
5.4. Over-sized		
6. Record Size		
6.1. One side		
6.2. Two-sides		
6.3. Single page		
6.4. Images 2-5		
6.5. Images 10-25		
6.6. Images 26-100		
6.7. Over 100		

Form 2: Records Considerations

RECORD KEEPING FACTOR	IMPACT	Weight
7. Quantity of Records		
7.1. Small		
7.2. Medium		
7.3. Large		
8. Value		
8.1. High operational value		
8.2. Vital record		
8.3. Short term		
8.4. Long term		
8.5. Difficult to replace		
9. Need to Integrate with Other Records		
9.1. Referral to many other records		
9.2. Predictable referral		
9.3. Unpredictable referral		
10. Quality		
10.1. Poor contrast		
10.2. Fragile		
10.3. Bent, ripped, torn		
11. Control Established		
11.1. During processing		
11.2. Active storage		
11.3. Inactive storage		
12. Active Use		
12.1. Long period		
12.2. High referral rate		
12.3. Low retrieval time		
13. Inactive Use		
13.1. Long period		
13.2. Longer referral rate		
13.3. High retrieval time		
14. Indexing Requirement		
14.1. No unique identifier		
14.2. Tied to existing data base		
14.3. Index containers only		
14.4. Index group (folders)		
14.5. Index each record		
14.6. No indexes		
14.7. Cross and multiple indexing		
15. Other		
15.1.		
15.2.		

Organizatonal Resources

Form 3 is used to evaluate the resources of the organization: people, infrastructure, and budget.

People

Almost everyone in an organization works with records in some capacity. However, the people involved with filing, retrieving, and converting records are generally the ones who are most directly responsible for the success of a system. Table 22 is a list of traits that are desirable for anyone who manages records. Those with checks are the ones essential for doing a good job of the tasks peculiar to a medium. The last column indicates the job traits needed to produce acceptable indexes, given separately because a computerized index can be made for any media. Most organizations do not reduce the number of employees as the result of a change in media. However, the structure and job skills required do change.

Working with paper records has very little, if any, prestige. The job is often part-time. Recordkeeping tasks are often divided among a number of people. Training programs are frequently inadequate because filing is generally considered an entry level job that anyone can do. Rarely is there an opportunity for advancement. This, combined with lack of recognition, means retaining employees can be a problem. Filing is a task where perfect performance merely meets expectations. Finding files is expected, only mistakes and omissions are noticed. Those who do get satisfaction from filing derive it internally — they meet their own standards.

Some of the same problems exist when the medium is microfilm. However, in most cases, the work is full-time. There may be little variety in tasks because each person specializes, in an effort to streamline production. In most cases document preparation takes much longer than the other tasks. It is a tedious task which requires that papers be sorted and arranged carefully — and some people do it full-time. Filming, developing, and processing are usually done by specialists with more training. The variety of tasks involved, along with the differences in training and skill needed, offers several levels of jobs. This gives employees a chance to progress beyond entry level duties. Most microfilm sections are separate from other work areas, so there is limited interaction with other employees.

The high-tech equipment of optical disk often confers a degree of prestige. Instead of just filing, a person works in a computer career field. Some of the difference is illusory, the tedious tasks of document preparation are still required. However, a good percentage of the work hours involve indexing. Clerical personnel may also be more involved in routine computer maintenance tasks. There is opportunity to train and advance. However, the work is very repetitive and an extremely high degree of accuracy is required. The pressures to turn around documents quickly with a very low error rate can be very high.

Factors 1.1 to 1.11 are used to evaluate the current records management staff's experience. Factors 1.1 to 1.5 should reflect the amount of experience with each medium and with indexing. Factors 1.6 to 1.8 measure the level of staff experience. A higher weight reflects more experience. Factors 1.9 to 1.11 measure the amount of experience the records management staff has with databases, computers, and conversion projects.

A score of 100 should be given to the relevant staff size (factor 2.1 to 2.4). This can be either the current staff or the desired staff level. As the number of workers are reduced there is pressure for each person to produce more. In records maintenance, this means the ratio of records maintained per worker increases. Regardless of the media, this ratio can usually be improved, but there are trade-offs. Paper requires the most labor. Some gains in efficiency can be made by changes in equipment, supplies, and work flow. After a certain point, either quality or service suffers. If the number of misfiles increases or people wait longer for records, the benefits of increased productivity turn into liabilities. Real increases in productivity, without sacrifices in quality and service, are easier to get from microfilm and optical disk systems. However, both microfilm and optical disk require a full-time staff. Rarely is the staff level under five people. Most of the staff time is required for document preparation and indexing.

Factors 3.1 and 3.2 measure the attitude of the records management staff towards change. While a positive attitude is not essential, it will make the transition and training easier.

Factors 4.1 through 6.2 measure the availability of in-house expertise and labor in the area of data processing. This expertise is valuable both in assessing and supporting systems. At a minimum, assistance will be needed in choosing a system. If support is not available in-house, the services of a consultant will be essential. If the in-house data processing

Table 22: Records Management Job Traits

Traits	Paper	Film	Optical	Index
Consistency	✔			✔
Adheres to established procedures	✔			✔
Takes initiative within parameters of job	✔			✔
Persistence	✔			
Sense of order and neatness	✔	✔		
Copes well with tedious tasks		✔		
Ability to perform very routine, repetitive tasks and maintain attention to detail	✔	✔	✔	✔
Understands functions of organization	✔			
Provides good customer service	✔			
Filming technical expertise		✔		
Expertise in developing and processing film		✔		
Extremely low tolerance of errors		✔		✔
Exercises judgement				✔
Can work under high pressure to produce			✔	✔
Maintain computer system			✔	✔
Backup data			✔	✔
Network management			✔	
Software expertise			✔	✔

staff is supportive, but busy, this is a workable alternative. However, if the attitude is hostile, the difficulty of establishing a strong system increases.

The attitudes, experiences, and needs of the users also play an important role in choosing a recordkeeping system. Part of the challenge of records management is that you manage what other people consider theirs. Making significant changes in the way records are managed, focuses attention on who owns the information. While legal ownership rests with the organization, individuals have power over, and responsibility for, records. The person with the power over the records often decides where it is kept and who can use it. This power is often assumed rather than assigned. The individual creator in particular may feel ownership. Someone who has spent a great deal of time writing a report or a computer program may feel it is theirs. Ownership may also be assumed by the segment of the organization that creates the records. For example, the manager of an engineering section may feel that the department owns all the blueprints.

Unfortunately, not everyone who assumes power over records assumes responsibility as well. The person responsible for records must see that they are properly cared for and, if they are not, that person shoulders the blame. This is a particular problem in organizations where records responsibility is not specifically assigned. Because responsibility is not assigned, it may be that no one is responsible. Poor recordkeeping practices may result. A vicious circle ensues. Because no one takes proper care of the records, people get more possessive, because information is not safe. The record system becomes increasingly fragmented and its management more difficult. Retention scheduling and adherence to legal requirements may be ignored. This is not a problem inherent in any particular medium, but a change in practices precipitated by a change in medium, may bring the problem to light. Often with a new system, control of the records generally changes hands. Power struggles may arise. While some managers may not particularly covet the headaches associated with recordkeeping, they do not want to relinquish power over their information.

The users' attitudes and their need for control over the records must be taken into consideration when choosing a medium. Factors 7.1.1 to 7.2.3 measure the filing tasks the users *want* to perform for themselves. Factors 7.1 and 7.2 are the degree of control the users want over active and inactive storage as a whole. Factors 8.1 to 8.3 measure where the user prefers to have active records located. The user's experi-

ence with database searches (9.1) and computers (9.2) is important when considering a change in medium. Factors 10.1 and 10.2 measure the user's attitude toward change.

The attitude of middle (11.1-11.4) and upper (12.1-12.3) management toward change is crucial. If support is not available, negative scores should be given. If both middle and upper management are strongly adverse to change, there is little likelihood of success for any system that is not traditional.

Paper does not *have* to be managed badly, it just is more likely to be. The effects of bad management show up slowly over time. People can build redundant systems and hoard their files. The costs of mismanagement are usually spread throughout the organization. It is hard to identify and quantify the costs of not having information when you want it, and it is easy to be ignorant of the costs. Even when intentions are good, it is easy to put problems off. Until a crisis occurs, problems with recordkeeping can be ignored. What is worse, few managers are taught to view records as assets that need to be managed and they are unlikely to recognize the efforts of those who do a good job of managing them.

Microfilm is likely to get more management attention, simply because it is easier to pinpoint costs and assess blame. How much attention it gets depends on where in the workflow the documents are converted. The earlier documents are converted the more attention the system gets because it impacts more directly and visibly on productivity.

Optical disk is likely to receive intense scrutiny by management. It incorporates new technologies and is very expensive. The more the system costs, the greater the expectations. Since optical disk systems are justified by anticipated improvements, this is not unreasonable. However, the increased attention on the part of upper level management is likely to include intense pressure to perform. Very rarely do optical disk systems wildly exceed expectations. When investing large amounts of money, expectations are already very high. Records managers do well to meet expectations.

Infrastructure

When considering the cost of a new system, it is important to evaluate the organization's current infrastructure. Often the largest equipment costs for an optical disk system are the work stations. If the organization already has much of the required hardware in place, the costs change dramatically, as does the training time. Other considerations are the organization's current equipment and standards. Factors 13.1 to 14.4 measure the degree to which the organization is standardized and how flexible those standards are. Factors 15.1 to 20.5 measure the equipment, space, and capacity available. The scores given in these areas also depend, to some degree, on how integrated a new system is expected to be. If little communication and interface is expected, then some of these factors may not apply. Those factors should be left blank.

A good infrastructure of equipment and wiring tends to make high tech solutions look more favorable. However, these same resources can be used to manage traditional media as well as the newer options. Infrastructure is only part of the overall picture when considering changes.

Funding

The amount and kinds of funds available for making changes are among the most significant factors. Regardless of how much a sophisticated microfilm or optical system could save, if there are no funds available to purchase the system, it cannot be implemented. However, the rating on these factors does not necessarily have to reflect what is in the budget, only what *could* be in the budget if an adequate job is done of persuading management that a change is called for.

Two types of funding need to be looked at — operating (21.1 to 21.3) and capital (22.1 to 22.5). The capital budget is generally a one-time infusion of funds while the operating budget is an annual figure. Often the goal is to trade-off a large one-time investment for a lower annual operating budget. This is a noble goal. It is not always possible. If recordkeeping is more centralized under the new system than the old, the operating and capital budgets are likely to increase. Management is often willing to make trade-offs between staffing levels and money. They are willing to buy a smaller staff with automation. Some reduction of staff is often possible. How much the staff can be reduced depends very much on the size of the current staff. If a very large central file room is maintained with large numbers of clerical personnel, reductions can be dramatic. If recordkeeping tasks are dispersed throughout the organization, and the records management staff is fairly small, there is not much opportunity to reduce the staff. In fact, the cost for the staff may increase. As the skill requirements increase, so do salaries. It is not realistic to expect to reduce the costs for the records management staff unless the current staff is quite large. Often the users, who have a different budget, will be the ones who save the most. In some instances, records management is understaffed and neglected, but personnel costs are low. When improvements are made, budget requirements increase. A realistic look must be taken at the budget. A well-designed system can usually produce more work with the same resources or the same work with fewer resources. Very rarely is more work with fewer resources possible.

Form 3: Organizational Resources

RECORDS SERIES		ORGANIZATIONAL COMPONENT	
ORGANIZATIONAL FACTOR		**WEIGHT**	**NOTES**
1. Records Mgmt (RM) Staff Experience			
1.1. Paper			
1.2. Microfilm			
1.3. Magnetic media			
1.4. Optical media			
1.5. Indexing			
1.6. Well-trained clerical			
1.7. Analytical			
1.8. Managerial			
1.9. Data base management			
1.10. Computer usage			
1.11. Project/Conversion management			
2. Size of RM Staff			
2.1. Small 1-5			
2.2. Medium 6-10			
2.3. Large 11-24			
2.4. Very large 25+			
3. Attitude of RM Staff			
3.1. Receptive to change			
3.2. Degree of support			
4. In-House Advice & Experience			
4.1. Distributed processing			
4.2. Network management			
4.3. Communication between systems			
4.4. Large database management			
4.5. Systems development			
5. Availability of Support From DP			
5.1. Distributed processing			
5.2. Network management			
5.3. Communication between systems			
5.4. Large database management			
5.5. Systems development			

Form 3: Organizational Resources

ORGANIZATIONAL FACTOR	WEIGHT	NOTES
6. Attitude of DP Staff		
6.1. Receptive to change		
6.2. Degree of support		
7. User's Preferred Filing Tasks		
7.1. Control over active storage		
7.1.1. Retrieval		
7.1.2. Filing		
7.1.3. Refiling		
7.2. Control over inactive storage		
7.2.1. Retrieval		
7.2.2. Filing		
7.2.3. Refiling		
8. Preferred Location: Active Records		
8.1. User's work area		
8.2. Adjacent to work area		
8.3. Central file area		
9. User's Experience		
9.1. Database searches		
9.2. Computer use		
10. User's Attitude		
10.1. Receptive to change		
10.2. Degree of support		
11. Middle Management		
11.1. Experience in managing change		
11.2. Receptive to change		
11.3. Degree of support		
11.4. Risk taker		
12. Upper Management		
12.1. Receptive to change		
12.2. Degree of support		
12.3. Risk taker		
13. Equipment Standards		
13.1. Commitment to org. standards		
13.2. Commitment to tech. standards		
13.3. Flexibility on standards		
13.4. Degree compatibility is required		

Form 3: Organizational Resources

ORGANIZATIONAL FACTOR	WEIGHT	NOTES
14. Media Standards & Commitment		
14.1. Commitment to current medium		
14.2. Commitment to tech. standards		
14.3. Flexibility on standards		
14.4. Degree compatibility is required		
15. Mainframe Infrastructure		
15.1. % of users supported		
15.2. % resources for user programs		
15.3. % support for RM		
15.4. % resources for RM programs		
15.5. Communication Ability		
15.6. Available capacity		
16. Network Infrastructure		
16.1. % of users supported		
16.2. % resources for user programs		
16.3. % support for RM		
16.4. % resources for RM		
16.5. Communication Ability		
16.6. Available capacity		
17. Wiring		
17.1. Network cabling in place		
17.2. Easy to add/upgrade		
18. Electronic Communications System		
18.1. Strained capacity		
18.2. Conventional capacity available		
18.3. High tech, high capacity		
19. Space		
19.1. High cost of space		
19.2. Pressure to reduce		
19.3. Maintain same space		
19.4. Expansion room available		
19.5. Expansion cost high		
20. Workstations (PC or UNIX)		
20.1. % of users supported		
20.2. Communication Ability		
20.3. VGA graphics or better		
20.4. Fast processor (286 or better)		
20.5. Large memory (RAM 2 meg +)		

Form 3: Organizational Resources

ORGANIZATIONAL FACTOR	WEIGHT	NOTES
21. Operating Budget Per Given Volume		
21.1. Must reduce		
21.2. Maintain current level		
21.3. Able to increase		
22. Capital Budget		
22.1. Under $50,000		
22.2. $ 50,001 - 150,000		
22.3. $150,001 - 250,000		
22.4. $250,001 - 1,000,000		
22.5. Over $1,000,000		
23. Other		
23.1.		
23.2.		
23.3.		
23.4.		
23.5.		
23.6.		
23.7.		
23.8.		

Section 9: Matching Needs and Media

This section contains a number of tables and forms to help match your organizational needs with the medium that is best suited for your application. However, these charts are of limited value unless they are applied to a specific set of records from a specific organization. This section is not as useful if you have not at least skimmed the material in the previous section. Also included are some ideas for mixing media and some compromises that can work when a change in media is not possible. The assessment forms and tables are valuable tools, but should not be used in a vacuum. The ratings given a medium represent the subjective opinions of the authors. The aspects of each medium are averaged and indicated in general. There are also many options within a medium. If one or more of the media have a similar score, then the medium is not nearly as important as how well the system is managed. Even when a medium is strongly indicated, the configuration and options within that medium are still open for choice.

Choosing a Storage Medium for Relational Data

There are really only two media that are well suited to storing large amounts of relational data — magnetic and optical. There are some simple paper-based note card systems but this is increasingly rare. Very seldom would most organizations consider paper as a viable medium for relational data. The alternatives are easier to use and more cost-effective. The primary trade-off between magnetic and optical media is speed versus volume. Magnetic media offers very quick access time. Optical media offers storage for extremely large volumes of data at a reasonable cost.

Table 23 lists the factors that go into choosing a medium for relational data. The second column is for the organization to assign a priority for that factor — much like the forms in the previous section. There are two columns each under Magnetic and Optical. Each has a rating assigned. This rating is the authors' assessment of how well the medium meets the needs for that factor. This is a qualitative assessment. Should you disagree with the assessment, change the rating. The weight is calculated by multiplying the organization's priority times the rating. The medium with the highest score will best suit the needs and priorities of the organization and information rated. There are two sections to the form: active data and backup data. It is very possible that magnetic media may be best suited for active data and optical best suited for backup data. If the scores are very close, then the choice of a medium is not particularly important.

Choosing a storage medium for relational data is rarely a records manager's task unless the information originates outside the data processing department. Many times a records manager will have to cope with storing old relational information. The challenges of storing the information may even call for conversion or backup to another medium.

Choosing a Storage Medium for Draft Records

Draft records exist primarily to become documents. Prior to the advent of word processing, drafts were not kept except as guide or form letters. Usually the problem with draft documents is *not* choosing a medium, but proper management. Many drafts are retained, but not as part of a program. Each individual author or typist keeps copies as they see fit. Too often the only time records managers become involved with draft documents is when diskettes are placed in storage with paper records. Like every other record, drafts need to be kept for a purpose, identified well, and destroyed when no longer needed. The only reason to keep electronic draft copies is to reuse them for creating new documents. If draft records are kept in place of documents, the recordkeeping system has problems. Draft records cannot legally substitute for an authenticated document.

A well-designed system can make very effective use of draft material. Table 24 lists some of the factors to consider in choosing between paper, magnetic, and optical media. This table is used in the same way as Table 23. You may wish to review the directions given above.

Choosing A Storage Medium For Documents

Documents constitute the bulk of most organizations' records. Because the primary function is to record and prove that actions have been taken or decisions made, these are the records that are most often used during disputes, audits, inspections, and legal proceedings. The other types of records: relational, draft, and publications, serve well-defined limited uses. But, while the basic purpose is the same, documents differ greatly in form and specific function. The choice of media is more complex. The same three forms that were used in the previous section to evaluate organizational needs are used to match those needs with a medium. Magnetic media are not considered. They are too volatile and easy to change to serve as a medium for documentation. The directions under relational data also apply to these forms.

Table 23: Choosing a Medium for Relational Data
Important: Review the directions before completing this form.

Record Series		Organizational Component			
Current Use			Magnetic		Optical
Factor	Priority	Rate	Weight	Rate	Weight
Data is very volatile		10		5	
Volume		2		10	
Quick access time		10		3	
Low equipment cost		8		-3	
Low media costs		2		8	
Equipment availability		7		-3	
Standardization		8		0	
Protection from change		-2		10	
Total					

Table 23 (Continued): Choosing a Medium for Relational Data

Backup Data		Magnetic		Optical	
Factor	Priority	Rate	Weight	Rate	Weight
Keep for long period		3		10	
Volume		5		10	
Equipment cost		2		-3	
Low media cost		3		8	
Standards		3		-5	
Equipment availability		5		-3	
Safety of data		-5		8	
No special environmental needs		-5		10	
Total					

Table 24: Choosing a Storage Medium for Draft Records

Important: Review the directions before completing this form.

Records Series	Organizational Component						
		Paper		Microfilm		Optical	
Management Concerns	Priority	Rate	Weight	Rate	Weight	Rate	Weight
1. Users							
1.1 Small group 1-5		8		10		5	
1.2 Medium 6-10		4		8		8	
1.3 Large 11-25		4		10		10	
1.4 Very Large 25+		5		10		8	
2. Usage							
2.1 Ad Hoc		5		-1		-10	
2.2 Formal		3		10		10	
2.3 Regular		1		10		10	
2.4 Sporadic		10		7		-10	
3. Rate of Update							
3.1 More than 6 times per year		3		10		5	
3.2 3 to 6 times per year		10		10		8	
3.3 1 to 2 times per year		5		5		10	

Records Series	Organizational Component						
		Paper		Microfilm		Optical	
Management Concerns	Priority						
4. Size of collection		Rate	Weight	Rate	Weight	Rate	Weight
4.1 Very small		10		10		2	
4.2 Medium		0		8		6	
4.3 Very Large		-10		4		10	
5. Equipment							
5.1 None		10		-10		-10	
5.2 In area		0		5		5	
5.3 On desktop		-10		10		10	
6. Percentage of repetitive work							
6.1 1-5%		5		10		-3	
6.2 6-15%		2		10		7	
6.3 16-30%		-8		10		8	
6.4 31-60%		-9		10		9	
6.5. 61% or more		-10		10		10	
7. Protection from changes		10		-10		10	
8. Program management							
8.1 None		6		3		-10	
8.2 Careful		5		8		8	
Total							

<h2 style="text-align:center">Form 4: Operational Concerns–Documents</h2>

IMPORTANT! Review the directions before completing this form.

Records Series	ORGANIZATIONAL COMPONENT					
		Paper		Microfilm		Optical
Management Concerns	Priority	Rate	Weight	Rate	Weight	Rate	Weight
1. Internal Distribution							
1.1. Speed		3		3		8	
1.2. Distance		3		3		6	
1.3. Reduce delays		3		3		8	
1.4. Accuracy of delivery		3		3		10	
2. Shipping/Mailing							
2.1. Bulk		2		8		9	
2.2. Quantity		3		9		6	
2.3. Distance		3		8		8	
2.4. Speed		3		6		7	
2.5. Safety		8		5		7	
2.6. Reduce delays in handling		3		5		7	
3. Electronic Distribution							
3.1. Graphics		6		6		9	
3.2. Machine-readable		1		1		1	
3.3. Quantity		1		1		3	
3.4. Person-to-person		10		8		10	
3.5. Place-to-place		10		8		7	
3.6. Speed		10		8		10	
4. Portability							
4.1. Used in-house		4		8		5	
4.2. Used by travelers		4		3		0	
5. Conversion Before Processing							
5.1. Turn-around		10		2		6	
6. Transaction Characteristics							
6.1. Value		4		6		10	
6.2. Quantity		4		8		10	
7. Transaction Life							
7.1. On-the-spot		1		1		10	
7.2. Under 4 hrs.		2		4		10	
7.3. Same day		5		8		10	
7.4. One - two days		6		8		8	
7.5. Two - five days		8		10		6	
7.6. Five - ten days		10		10		0	
7.7. Over 10 days		10		5		0	

Form 4: Operational Concerns–Documents

Management Concerns	Priority	Paper		Microfilm		Optical	
		Rate	Weight	Rate	Weight	Rate	Weight
8. No. of People Involved in Processing							
8.1. Very small 1-2		10		9		9	
8.2. Small 3-8		7		9		10	
8.3. Medium 9-64		5		9		10	
8.4. Large 64 or more		3		6		10	
8.5. Well-defined		5		0		10	
8.6. Unpredictability		10		7		2	
9. Type of Task							
9.1. Well-defined		10		10		10	
9.2. Unpredictable		10		3		5	
9.3. Sequential processing		10		10		10	
9.4. Parallel processing		2		2		10	
10. Access							
10.1. Easy to find directly		4		5		9	
10.2. Good cross-reference		3		4		8	
10.3. Speed		2		7		10	
11. Simultaneous access							
11.1. Number of People		2		10		8	
11.2. Speed		1		3		10	
11.3. Copy Consistency		2		10		10	
11.4. Cost		5		10		1	
12. Access Restrictions							
12.1. Low number of people		8		6		8	
12.2. Degree of confidentiality		6		8		10	
13. Dispersion of Work group							
13.1. Same floor		8		6		10	
13.2. Same building		5		5		9	
13.3. Same complex		3		3		7	
13.4. Remote access needed		3		1		5	
14. Record Ergonomics							
14.1. Multiple records viewed		10		0		3	
14.2. Large record size		10		1		2	
14.3. Working comfort		10		2		4	
14.4. Portability		10		4		1	
15. Processing Safety							
15.1. Resistance to handling		5		10		10	
15.2. Environmental requirements		8		10		6	
15.3. Disaster resistance		3		10		8	

Form 4: Operational Concerns–Documents

Management Concerns	Priority	Paper		Microfilm		Optical	
		Rate	Weight	Rate	Weight	Rate	Weight
16. Standard Practices							
16.1. Equipment used		6		10		3	
16.2. Identification of information		1		8		4	
16.3. Retrieval processes		1		8		5	
17. Equipment to use records							
17.1. Availability of equipment		10		6		2	
17.2. Speed		2		8		10	
17.3. Cost of equipment		10		4		1	
17.4. Compatibility		10		1		5	
17.5. Integration w. other equipment		0		2		8	
17.6. Reliability of access		10		7		3	
17.7. Skill level needed		10		8		6	
18. Integrity of Information							
18.1. Misfile		2		8		8	
18.2. Loss		3		10		10	
18.3. Degree of fragmentation		2		5		9	
18.4. Ease of refiling		1		10		10	
18.5. Control		1		6		10	
19. Accuracy of Information							
19.1. Low error rate		6		8		9	
19.2. Current		6		8		10	
19.3. Consistent		4		10		10	
19.4. Speed of updates		2		8		10	
20. Use of Information							
20.1. Work group only		10		10		10	
20.2. Departmental		5		10		8	
20.3. Organization wide		5		10		2	
20.4. Shared with customers/clients		8		9		1	
20.5. Public information		10		8		0	
21. Data Input							
21.1. Part of process		3		0		10	
21.2. Relates directly to records		2		6		10	
22. Alteration							
22.1. Need to authenticate		10		-10		-10	
22.2. Change existing documents		10		-8		-3	
22.3. Add to existing records		10		2		8	
23. Copies							
23.1. Very small: 2-10		10		8		10	
23.2. Small: 11-49		6		10		10	
23.3. Moderate: 50-100		3		10		6	

Form 4: Operational Concerns–Documents

Management Concerns	Priority	Paper		Microfilm		Optical	
		Rate	Weight	Rate	Weight	Rate	Weight
23.4. Large: over 100		2		10		6	
23.5. Consistency among copies		3		10		10	
23.6. Low turn-around time		3		8		10	
24. Legal Acceptability							
24.1. Audit Trail		10		9		7	
24.2. Trustworthiness		10		9		7	
24.3. Well-tested		10		9		-5	
25. Limited Training Requirements							
25.1. Records management basics		8		4		7	
25.2. Equipment use		10		5		2	
26. Active Storage							
26.1. Equipment cost		8		6		2	
26.2. Space reduction		2		10		10	
26.3. Higher capacity		2		10		6	
26.4. Expansion potential		2		10		6	
26.5. Proximity		6		8		10	
26.6. Length of time		6		10		4	
26.7. Environmental requirements		5		10		6	
26.8. Disaster resistance		3		10		8	
27. Inactive Storage							
27.1. Equipment cost		10		8		2	
27.2. Space reduction		5		10		10	
27.3. Higher capacity		5		10		8	
27.4. Expansion potential		5		10		8	
27.5. Proximity		2		8		6	
27.6. Length of time		9		10		1	
27.7. Environmental requirements		2		10		6	
27.8. Disaster resistance		2		10		8	
28. Other							
28.1.							
28.2.							
28.3.							
28.4.							
28.5.							
28.6.							
28.7.							
28.8.							
28.9.							
28.10							
TOTAL							

Form 5: Record Considerations–Documents

IMPORTANT! Review the directions before completing this form.

RECORDS SERIES	Organizational Component						
RECORD KEEPING FACTOR	**Priority**	**PAPER**		**MICROFILM**		**OPTICAL**	
		Rate	Weight	Rate	Weight	Rate	Weight
1. Record Creation							
1.1. Skill required		10		3		5	
1.2. Equipment cost		10		5		5	
1.3. Equipment availability		10		8		5	
1.4. Turn around time		6		10		10	
1.5. Accuracy		5		10		10	
1.6. Reusability of old copy		8		3		3	
1.7. Initiated by organization		9		8		8	
1.8. Reaction		10		4		5	
2. Conversion							
2.1. Turn around		10		4		6	
2.2. Before processing		10		2		5	
2.3. After processing		10		7		7	
2.4. Preparation required		10		5		6	
3. Type of Record							
3.1. Unitized		7		4		6	
3.2. Transactional		8		8		10	
3.3. Reference		7		4		6	
4. Retention Period							
4.1. Keep under 6 months		10		2		4	
4.2. Keep 6 months - 2 yrs.		10		6		10	
4.3. Keep 2-5 yrs.		10		8		8	
4.4. Keep 6-10 yrs.		10		10		5	
4.5. Keep 11-20 yrs.		8		10		2	
4.6. Keep 21-50 yrs.		7		10		-2	
4.7. Keep 51-100 yrs.		3		10		-5	
4.8. Keep over 100 yrs.		2		9		-10	
5. Size							
5.1. Uniform		10		10		10	
5.2. Mixed		8		7		6	
5.3. Legal size or less		10		10		10	
5.4. Over-sized		9		6		2	
6. Record Size							
6.1. One side		10		10		10	
6.2. Two-sides		8		8		6	
6.3. Single page		10		10		10	
6.4. Images 2-9		10		10		9	
6.5. Images 10-25		10		9		5	
6.6. Images 26-100		10		8		2	
6.7. Over 100		10		7		1	

Form 5: Record Considerations–Documents

RECORD KEEPING FACTOR	PRIORITY	Paper		Microfilm		Optical	
		Rate	Weight	Rate	Weight	Rate	Weight
7. Quantity of Records							
7.1. Small		10		8		9	
7.2. Medium		9		8		8	
7.3. Large		6		8		6	
8. Value							
8.1. High operational value		4		6		10	
8.2. Vital record		3		10		6	
8.3. Short term		5		10		10	
8.4. Long term		6		10		0	
8.5. Difficult to replace		2		10		9	
9. Need to Integrate with Other Records							
9.1. Referral to many other records		5		5		8	
9.2. Predictable referral		6		6		9	
9.3. Unpredictable referral		6		6		7	
10. Quality							
10.1. Poor contrast		8		6		3	
10.2. Fragile		8		5		3	
10.3. Bent, ripped, torn		8		5		3	
11. Control Established							
11.1. During processing		2		3		9	
11.2. Active storage		4		7		7	
11.3. Inactive storage		6		10		3	
12. Active Use							
12.1. Long period		6		10		8	
12.2. High referral rate		4		7		9	
12.3. Low retrieval time		4		8		10	
13. Inactive Use							
13.1. Long period		8		10		1	
13.2. High referral rate		4		6		7	
13.3. Low retrieval time		2		5		8	
14. Indexing Requirement							
14.1. No unique identifier		10		5		2	
14.2. Tied to existing data base		4		8		8	
14.3. Index containers only		8		8		-10	
14.4. Index group (folders)		10		8		4	
14.5. Index each record		3		9		10	
14.6. No indexes		8		6		-10	
14.7. Cross and multiple indexing		4		8		10	
15. Other							
15.1.							
15.2.							
15.3.							
TOTAL							

Form 6: Organizational Resources–Documents

IMPORTANT! Review the directions before completing this form.

RECORDS SERIES	ORGANIZATIONAL COMPONENT					
	Avail. or PRIORITY	Paper		Microfilm		Optical
OPERATIONAL FACTOR		Rate	Weight	Rate	Weight	Rate	Weight
1. Records Mgmt (RM) Staff Experience							
1.1. Paper		10		8		6	
1.2. Microfilm		0		10		3	
1.3. Magnetic media		3		6		10	
1.4. Optical media		0		0		10	
1.5. Indexing		6		6		10	
1.6. Well-trained clerical		6		8		10	
1.7. Analytical		5		8		8	
1.8. Managerial		3		8		10	
1.9. Database management		3		6		10	
1.10. Computer usage		3		6		10	
1.11. Project/Conversion management		3		10		10	
2. Size of RM Staff							
2.1. Small 1-5		6		2		2	
2.2. Medium 6-10		8		5		5	
2.3. Large 11-24		6		10		10	
2.4. Very large 25+		5		8		7	
3. Attitude of RM Staff							
3.1. Receptive to change		3		6		8	
3.2. Degree of support		5		8		10	
4. In-House Advice & Experience							
4.1. Distributed processing		0		2		7	
4.2. Network management		0		3		8	
4.3. Communication between systems		0		7		10	
4.4. Large database management		2		7		10	
4.5. Systems development		5		2		10	
5. Availability of Support From DP							
5.1. Distributed processing		0		2		8	
5.2. Network management		0		3		10	
5.3. Communication between systems		0		8		8	
5.4. Large database management		2		5		8	
5.5. Systems development		5		6		8	

Form 6: Organizational Resources–Documents

OPERATIONAL FACTOR	PRIORITY	Paper		Microfilm		Optical	
		Rate	Weight	Rate	Weight	Rate	Weight
6. Attitude of DP Staff							
6.1. Receptive to change		0		5		8	
6.2. Degree of support		2		5		8	
7. User's Preferred Filing Tasks							
7.1. Control over active storage		10		3		8	
7.1.1. Retrieval		6		4		10	
7.1.2. Filing		10		0		3	
7.1.3. Refiling		10		0		0	
7.2. Control over inactive storage		5		3		7	
7.2.1. Retrieval		4		4		6	
7.2.2. Filing		6		0		0	
7.2.3. Refiling		4		0		0	
8. Preferred Location: Active Records							
8.1. User's work area		9		3		8	
8.2. Adjacent to work area		6		8		4	
8.3. Central file ares		9		10		2	
9. User's Experience							
9.1. Database searches		3		6		10	
9.2. Computer use		1		6		10	
10. User's Attitude							
10.1. Receptive to change		0		6		7	
10.2. Degree of support		3		5		8	
11. Middle Management							
11.1. Experience in managing change		0		5		7	
11.2. Receptive to change		3		6		8	
11.3. Degree of support		4		7		10	
11.4. Risk taker		2		5		10	
12. Upper Management							
12.1. Receptive to change		2		6		10	
12.2. Degree of support		4		6		10	
12.3. Risk taker		0		6		10	
13. Equipment Standards							
13.1. Commitment to org. standards		5		10		7	
13.2. Commitment to tech. standards		0		10		7	
13.3. Flexibility on standards		0		3		10	
13.4. Degree compatibility is required		10		7		2	

Form 6: Organizational Resources–Documents

OPERATIONAL FACTOR	PRIORITY	Paper		Microfilm		Optical	
		Rate	Weight	Rate	Weight	Rate	Weight
14. Media Standards & Commitment							
14.1. Commitment to current medium		1		1		1	
14.2. Commitment to tech. standards		0		10		2	
14.3. Flexibility on standards		0		0		10	
14.4. Degree compatibility is required		10		10		1	
15. MainFrame Infrastructure							
15.1. % of users supported		0		3		7	
15.2. % resources for user programs		0		0		-5	
15.3. % support for RM		1		3		7	
15.4. % resources for RM programs		1		3		8	
15.5. Communication Ability		0		1		6	
15.6. Available capacity		1		2		10	
16. Network Infrastructure							
16.1. % of users supported		0		5		10	
16.2. % resources for user programs		0		0		-5	
16.3. % support for RM		1		5		10	
16.4. % resources for RM		1		5		10	
16.5. Communication Ability		0		3		10	
16.6. Available capacity		0		5		10	
17. Wiring							
17.1. Network cabling in place		0		4		10	
17.2. Easy to add/upgrade		0		3		7	
18. Electronic Communications System							
18.1. Strained capacity		4		1		-3	
18.2. Conventional capacity available		2		2		1	
18.3. High tech, high capacity		0		3		10	
19. Space							
19.1. High cost of space		-2		10		10	
19.2. Pressure to reduce		-10		10		10	
19.3. Maintain same space		-5		8		8	
19.4. Expansion room available		2		3		3	
19.5. Expansion cost high		-5		10		10	
20. Workstations (PC or UNIX)							
20.1. % of users supported		0		5		10	
20.2. Communication Ability		0		3		10	
20.3. VGA graphics or better		0		3		10	
20.4. Fast processor (286 or better)		0		3		10	
20.5. Large memory (RAM 2 meg +)		0		2		10	

Form 6: Organizational Resources–Documents

OPERATIONAL FACTOR	PRIORITY	PAPER		MICROFILM		OPTICAL	
		Rate	Weight	Rate	Weight	Rate	Weight
21. Operating Budget Per Given Volume							
21.1. Must reduce		-10		10		7	
21.2. Maintain current level		-5		10		10	
21.3. Able to increase		5		3		4	
22. Capital Budget							
22.1. Under $50,000		10		-3		-10	
22.2. $ 50,001 - 150,000		10		7		-5	
22.3. $150,001 - 250,000		0		8		0	
22.4. $250,001 - 1,000,000		0		10		6	
22.5. Over $1,000,000		0		10		8	
23. Other							
23.1.							
23.2.							
23.3.							
23.4.							
23.5.							
23.6.							
23.7.							
23.8.							
TOTAL							

Choosing a Medium for Publications

Paper, microfilm, and optical media, in particular CD-ROM, are possible media for publications. The decision is not as complex as that for documents, but more complex than choosing a medium for drafts and relational information. Table 25 lists factors that should be considered and the impact each medium has upon that factor. It may also be helpful to review Section 4 on CD-ROM, which discusses the use of CD-ROM for publications in detail.

Acting On Your Decision

Once you have used the forms and tables above and chosen the medium most likely to succeed, what next? The answer depends on whether a change is indicated, what the change is, and the extent of the problems with the current system. Too often a change in medium is used to solve problems that are not so much with the medium as the management and control of the current system. A large investment in equipment and software cannot substitute for good management. In fact, a change in medium can magnify the extent of management deficiencies. A change in medium is often an opportunity to improve management practices. Regardless of whether or not a change of media is indicated, recordkeeping policies and practices should be well documented; the records staff well trained; forms and reports should be evaluated to determine what can be eliminated or combined; efforts should be made to reduce and eliminate unneeded duplicate copies of records wherever possible; and a good, current, well-enforced retention schedule should be in place. These practices are important, regardless of the medium. Generally, improvement can be made in these areas without a change in media.

Within the constraints of any media, there are many options. Visits to trade shows, case studies, publications, seminars, and ideas from other professionals will help develop a range of options. The Association of Records Managers and Administrators, Inc. (ARMA International) and the Association of Information and Image Management (AIIM) are good sources of all of the above. Especially valuable is contact with fellow professionals who can offer the benefit of their experience and assistance. Vendors are often a source of valuable assistance — particularly in educating you about the range of equipment and software available. The best vendors will help analyze and implement your system, as your continued success is important to their continued relationship. Care must be taken in comparing and choosing vendors. When more technical applications are being reviewed, it is wise to form an in-house task group that draws on in-house expertise. However, it is also important that the evaluations and decisions focus on functionality and the ability to meet the organization's needs. Many of the systems available are truly awe-inspiring, but the features that are intriguing and fascinating may have little or no applicability. If the people evaluating the system do not have a clear picture of the organization's needs, they can be distracted and enchanted by features that may have limited value. Also, avoid choosing a system that over-solves your problem. When 25% of the system solves 1% of the problem, it is too expensive. The process of evaluating and weighing organizational needs helps avoid buying an alluring system and then finding something to do with it.

In some cases a committee can provide the mix of talent and support needed to see a project through. If major changes are being made, consider hiring a consultant. In addition to providing technical assistance, a consultant can also help to ensure that all the endless details of assessing systems, making decisions, and implementing changes are seen to. The process is often very time consuming and may be difficult to accomplish along with ongoing job requirements. When a large number of records must be converted, a service bureau may be an efficient and economical alternative, particularly when the conversion schedule is short.

Current Medium Is Indicated

If the medium indicated is the one currently being used, you may need to analyze and improve the current system. An evaluation of organizational needs and priorities will help focus on the areas where improvements are needed. If the current system is not sufficient, more pervasive changes may be needed. Sometimes a system that suffices rather than the one that is optimal, is the only option from the standpoint of budgetary constraints. A good records management software program can be helpful regardless of the medium. Often a modest investment in equipment and software can have a large impact. Indexing software in particular can help with the difficult problem of control and retrieval of records. The challenge, in any case, is to build strength in the most critical areas, without weakening the total system. Creativity, well-designed and implemented procedures, and good training often substitute well for an investment in new equipment.

Table 25: Choosing a Medium for Publications

Factor	Paper	Microfilm	Optical
Material preparation The effort required to get material ready for publication.	Most office systems are geared to producing paper output. Cut and paste techniques allow the incorporation of a great deal of material.	The material preparation steps are the same as for paper.	This is generally the most expensive step for optical, getting all information in machine-readable format. If the information is already machine-readable, then this step is simple.
Mastering costs The cost of producing a master copy for originals.	No additional costs.	Roll microfilm requires document preparation and filming. Most publications are distributed on microfiche. In this case, jacket fiche must be prepared on a step-and-repeat camera used for making a master. Computer output microfilm can also be used for publishing.	Prior to mastering, the document must be authored. CD-ROM is the most common optical format used for publishing. A master disk is made. The cost of mastering varies greatly, depending on the vendor, the number of copies, and the relationship with the vendor.
Duplicating costs	From 2¢ to 5¢ per image, depending on the quality of paper and quantity.	Costs are very low, between $7 and $12 per roll and about 25¢ per fiche.	CD-ROM copies range from $2 to $55 each. Other optical media can be used, but it must be copied just like magnetic disk.
Mailing costs	Mailing costs can be quite high. The weight and bulk of paper often requires shipping.	Costs are low due to reduced bulk.	Bulk and weight are reduced to a minimal amount. However, because of the high value, special handling is often used.

Table 25 (Continued): Choosing a Medium for Publications

Factor	Paper	Microfilm	Optical
Updating Many publications need to be updated on a regular basis. The frequency and volume of the updates are important factors in choosing a medium.	Paper publications can be updated by additions and changes. However, if the number of publications is large, such as regulations, keeping the publications posted and updated is a time consuming task.	Publications on microfilm are usually replaced by a new, revised copy. This eliminates the need for posting changes. However, the entire publication generally must be reprinted and remastered.	Optical disk publications are usually updated with replacement. The cost and capacity make them impractical for small addendums. Complete replacements are possible.
User base The number of users, the predictability of who they are, and how closely they are associated with the organization are factors to consider in choosing a publication medium.	Paper is the medium that presents the fewest barriers to use. It is particularly useful where the size and composition of the audience varies. The more public the audience, the more likely it is that paper will be the medium of choice.	Microfilm is very accessible to most organizations and institutions. Particularly when the user base is very large, microfilm is an attractive alternative.	Optical media are the least accessible to users because of equipment restrictions. However, most libraries and many organizations have, or are adding, CD-ROM readers. For some audiences and publications, CD-ROM is an excellent alternative.
User equipment Microfilm and optical disk require special equipment to use.	Paper requires no special equipment to use. It can easily be used in a central library or the individual work area.	Microfiche and microfilm readers are available in most organizations and institutions. However, they may not be available at the user's desk. When evaluating the availability of equipment and its impact, the function of the publication needs to be taken into consideration.	The same considerations as those for microfilm need to be taken into account. Optical disk publications are very well-suited for very frequent lookups. The indexing can be very powerful. It offers very quick access to a large body of information, in a way that no other medium can.

Table 25 (Continued): Choosing a Medium for Publications

Factor	Paper	Microfilm	Optical
Portability needs Some publications need to travel. For example, one that describes inventory parts may need to be taken to the warehouse to match a part with a picture.	Paper is the most portable of all the media. It is easy to carry in small quantities, and requires no special equipment to use.	Microfiche, in particular, can be relatively portable. Special viewers are needed, but they are available. Small excerpts can be printed out and taken along. Microfilm may be the best medium when very large publications need to be carried along.	Optical media is the least portable of the media. Many CD-ROM drives are available for personal computers and could conceivably be taken to the field. This is not yet common. The equipment is not common and is expensive compared to the other options.
Nature of information The type of information and how it is used should be carefully considered when choosing a medium.	Publications that are meant to be read once and then rarely referred to again, are well suited to paper. Some examples are newsletters, periodic activity reports, and information that is timer sensitive. Also well-suited to paper are publications that have passages that need to be compared to passages in other records. Papers can be laid side-by-side for comparison.	Microfilm is best suited to publications for occasional reference to selected portions, particularly those that are very lengthy. It is also an economical way to provide a large library in a reduced amount of space.	Optical media offer the ability to mix text, graphics, and data with a powerful database index. It is also well suited to voluminous information. Since the information is machine-readable but not subject to change, optical media is a good medium for publications that have information designed to be incorporated into other records.

A Different Medium Is Indicated

If a medium different from the current one is indicated, the first step is *not* to contact vendors, but to more carefully examine your current system. Which needs are directly related to recordkeeping practices and which are directly linked to the choice of media? The question of conversion is one of the most difficult. Carefully consider the point in the life cycle where the records are best converted. If a change can be made from the implementation date forward, this is the best option because there is no need to convert a large backlog. It may be helpful to evaluate older records on a separate form, making a separate media decision for those records. Massive conversions are very time-consuming. Most organizations will want to staff for current operations. A large conversion means a choice of overtaxing the system at a point when the staff is most inexperienced and stressed; adding staff and equipment that may not be needed after the conversion; or using a service bureau. In any case management will have to control two very different processes; increasing the stresses and difficulties. Many times a change in medium coincides with a sharp improvement in recordkeeping practices. In this case the conversion process requires paying the price not only for the changes in medium, but for the correction of past deficiencies as well. A system that mixes old and new media may be the best answer: keep the old records on the current medium and convert only from the implementation forward. In other cases, a partial conversion may be possible converting only those older records that are referred to on a regular basis. The alternatives need to be carefully researched.

Once the problem of a conversion is addressed, the search for a system can begin. As was pointed out above, the focus should be how well the needs of the organization are met, not which system has the most, and best, features. Evaluate the systems against the organization's yardstick, not against each other.

Mixing Media

Often a mix of media works better than a single medium. One reason the concept of a paperless office enjoyed so much press in the early 1980's was because of the appeal of a simple, clean solution to all our perplexing paper problems. By this point, it should be apparent that many of those perplexing problems have nothing to do with the medium, they have more to do with the complexity of dealing with recorded information and the infinite number of ways it can be used. Since the best choice of media depends on the needs of the organization and the function of the information, it is likely that the best choice for many organizations will be a mix of media. While the stacks of paper may diminish greatly, there is still no other medium that is as easy to use. Printers are important components of both microfilm and optical disk systems. Anything other than 100% paper is already a hybrid system.

It is also not necessary to have a single database that links all the possible information in the organization. In some ways this has replaced the dream of a paperless office. It has the same major failing as it attempts to treat unequal assets equally. A good records management program will plan an overall system where different types of records are treated as parts of a whole. Records should receive a share of resources and management time that reflects their importance to the organization. Some sub-systems will need to be compatible or linked. Others may standalone. Additionally, records and information needs are dynamic. A good solution for today may not work in two years. Automation cannot substitute for good management. Simplistic or idealistic systems work only in simple or ideal situations.

Living With Compromises and Making Them Work

Sometimes it is clear that a new medium would be very beneficial, but for some reason, usually inadequate capital or management resistance, conversion is not possible within the near future. If there are serious weaknesses in the current system, do not wait for the miracle of conversion. Many of the problems are very likely related to management practices rather than media constraints. Rarely does a system exist that only a change in media can remedy. Improving the current system will often serve to enhance both your credibility and the chances for future changes. Lay the groundwork while biding your time. First, become well acquainted with the strengths and weaknesses of the desired medium. Do another careful assessment of your current system. Reduce the size of the records collection as much as possible. Be sure the current retention schedule is enforced. Use the evaluation forms to help pinpoint areas that are most important to the success of your system and work on those. A transition plan that meets economic, recordkeeping, and management needs will increase the chances for success. Long-term budgeting plans may allow for obtaining equipment within financial constraints. Plan changes that will enhance the current system while moving towards the new one. For example, if reducing index needs through bar coding is part of the plan for the new system, add bar codes to new and reprinted forms. The quality of both microfilm and optical media is enhanced when the contrast between printing and background are maximized. Changing the color of papers may also be done as forms are devised and revised. Often the system for finding records, classification and arrangement, can be improved dramatically. These changes will be beneficial regardless of the medium used. Section 5 addresses some of the factors that need to be taken into consideration.

Technology does not eliminate any options, it only adds them. Technology offers the opportunity to build marvelous, efficient systems. It also offers the opportunity to build costly, clumsy monsters. More options increase the importance of good management. Become acquainted with the new tools and learn to use them wisely.

Section 10: Approving a Change in Medium

When approving a change in medium, management must be concerned about the effectiveness of the overall organization and the best allotment of resources within operating constraints. While changing a system may improve it, improvement is not automatic. The more dramatic the change, the more careful the planning for this change should be. This section is designed to help management review and evaluate requests that involve changing to a different medium. Information from other sections is summarized and presented in an overview. This section can be used alone, without references to other parts of this publication. However, if the planned change is dramatic or costly, it may be advantageous to review this publication more thoroughly. Table 26 is an evaluation form. Each factor is evaluated as meeting the requirement (yes), not meeting it (no), or as not being applicable or important for the case under consideration (n/a). There are no set rules for how many evaluation factors must be met. This is a judgement call for management. A large number of *no* answers, or *no* answers in any critical areas, may indicate more planning and investigation are needed prior to approval.

Table 26: Request Evaluation: Change in Medium

Evaluation Factor	Yes	No	N/A
Why Change			
1. Knowledge of current system			
1.1. Number and type of records			
1.2. Growth rate			
1.3. Who uses the records and how			
1.4. Problems that need to be corrected			
1.5. User's needs and priorities			
2. Institutionalize decision making			
2.1. Enforces consistency			
2.2. Requires less routine intervention by managers			
3. Competitive advantage			
3.1. Time compression			
3.2. Better service			
3.3. Better internal information			

Evaluation Factor	Yes	No	N/A
Fits Organization			
1. Mission of organization			
1.1. Shows knowledge of overall goals & plans			
1.2. Fits into overall needs			
1.3. Complements mission			
2. Standardization			
2.1 Fits current standards			
2.2. Sets acceptable standards			
3. Infrastructure			
3.1. Equipment base exists to support changes			
3.1. Adjustment of equipment base is acceptable			
4. Flexible			
4.1. Can accommodate growth			
4.2. Can accommodate change			
5. Migration			
5.1. Index information can be moved to new system			
5.2. Uses standard file structurer or converts easily			

Evaluation Factor	Yes	No	N/A
Resource Requirements			
1. Capital expenditure			
1.1. Costs fully considered			
1.2. Costs projected over life of project			
1.3. Savings projected carefully			
2. Personnel			
2.1. Realistic assessment of cost savings			
2.2. Changes well-planned			
2.3. Training needs considered			
3. Space			
3.1. Actual space savings shown			
3.2. Time table			
4. Costs proportionate to value			

Table 26: (Continued)
Request Evaluation: Change in Medium

Evaluation Factor	Yes	No	N/A
Solution Selected			
1. Solutions considered			
1.1. Due consideration given number of alternatives			
1.2. Two to five vendors seriously considered			
2. Based on organization's priorities and needs			
2.1. Needs and priorities set in advance			
2.2. Vendors measured against needs			
2.3. Not compared solely on features			
3. Entire solution is needed			
4. Vendor			
4.1. Proprietary equipment & software			
4.2. Acceptable experience base			

Evaluation Factor	Yes	No	N/A
Potential Problem Areas			
1. Indexing			
1.1. Index has been sized			
1.2. Number of keystrokes per person reasonable			
1.3. Methods to reduce keystrokes explored			
1.4. Edits and corrections easily made			
2. Conversion			
2.1. Needed			
2.2. Well-planned			
2.3. Impact on new program carefully assessed			
3. Adequate time allowed for document preparation			
Medium Selected			
1. Life of system matches life of records			
2. Strengths of medium match needs			

Reasons To Change

The reasons for making the change are key. The reasons should show a clear understanding of the organization and its priorities. On rare occasions the right changes can be made for the wrong reasons, but as the complexity and cost of the system increase, the chances of this become increasingly remote.

- *Knowledge of the current system.* How well has the current system been analyzed? Records management systems are rarely neat and tidy. If the current system is not well understood, then the problems it causes may not be understood either. Rarely are unrecognized problems inadvertently solved with a new system. More often, hidden problems are the reason a new system either fails or costs more than projected. Changes should be in response to fundamental problems. The proposed system should be able to fix these problems without causing additional problems. The solution should be in direct proportion to the problem.

- *Number and type of records.* Determining the number and characteristics of records is often difficult. It is important that proper sampling techniques be used to determine the total number of images, the number of two-sided records, the dimensions of the records, the physical condition, and the amount of preparation required if filmed or scanned. This is essential. The size of the system and staff are built upon the size of the record collection. Poor data in this area will lead to poor planning. It could result in the purchase of a system that is too small to accommodate the records it is designed for.

- *Growth rate.* Record collections tend to grow exponentially. The historical growth rate and factors that affect the growth of records over the system life should be taken into consideration. The system must either be sized to allow for this growth or the plans made to expand as needed. The costs for foreseeable expansion should be included in the cost of the system.

- *Who uses records and how.* The purpose and function of the records need to be served by the new medium. If the records are used by others outside the organization, this must also be taken into consideration.

- *Problems that need to be corrected.* Plans for changing media should be preceded by very careful identification and analysis of problems with the current system.

- *User's needs and priorities.* Records systems need to be designed for the users. Their needs and priorities should take precedence in most cases. Designing the system to fit with other systems or to make life easier for records management is acceptable, but only if the user's needs take precedence. Fulfilling user needs is the primary justification for changes.

- *Institutionalized Decision-Making.* Designing uniformity into the system can also institutionalize decision-making. This frees managers to make decisions by exception rather than on a routine basis.

- *Enforces consistency.* Some systems force uniformity into a recordkeeping system. For example, a computerized index that requires certain fields will guarantee that specified information is kept for all items in the index.

- *Requires less routine intervention by managers.* In organizations with poor recordkeeping systems, middle or top management must participate in routine records management decisions. For example, if records are not routinely classified by the recordkeeping system, records stack up until a manager has time to go through the records and classify each individually — a poor use of management time.

- *Competitive advantage.* In some cases, a change in medium can help an organization greatly improve its performance in a way that will make customers happier: increasing satisfaction, generating and repeat business, and decreasing complaints.

- *Time compression.* Particularly when the records in question are part of a transaction process, a new medium may help reduce the time required to process the transaction. This allows the same staff to handle more work, decreases backlogs, or even allows staff reductions. Optical disk systems, in particular, have been successful in this area.

- *Better service.* When better customer service means having faster access to records, a change in medium can lead to significant improvements. If requests are made over the phone or in person, magnetic and optical media are the fastest. If the retrieval time allowed is over twenty minutes, then microfilm and some paper systems can give satisfactory results.

- *Better internal information.* Better internal information can mean cross-indexing, fast access and retrieval, or improved file integrity. The value of the improvement depends on the importance and value of the transaction supported.

Fits Organization

The solution should fit the organization: its purpose, structure, and future plans.

- *Mission of the Organization.* Each organization has a reason for being. The recordkeeping system must be designed with that mission in mind and complement it. The Mormon Church's selection of jacket microfiche as a medium for genealogical records is an excellent example of how a medium can enhance the mission of an organization. The original roll film can be archived for hundreds of years. The fiche are quickly and easily duplicated. The regional research centers can have a full set of microfiche at a reasonable cost.

- *Standardization.* How well does the system fit with the rest of the organization and its customers? If the organization has chosen a standard workstation and the proposed solution is not compatible, there should either be a strong justification for the deviation or a reappraisal of the standard. Standards increase in importance with the impact of the records. A small, stand-alone system that has limited impact on the rest of the organization may be acceptable. At the same time, a system that impacts many people in the organization or its customers must meet more rigorous standards.

- *Infrastructure.* Optical systems that store images require a heavy investment in equipment and wiring. New microfilm reader/printers are currently being developed that can also digitize images and transmit them to work stations. These will also require image capable work stations and wiring capable of handling very large files. If these requirements have already been met, the investment is much less. If the upgraded infrastructure can

meet other requirements or fits into an overall master plan, then it is easier to justify the expense and plan for expansion.

- *Flexibility.* Take into consideration how often the organization changes structure and work goals. How easy is it to rearrange the recordkeeping system to reflect organizational changes?

- *Migration.* No system is so wonderful that it will work forever. The ability to grow and change should be built in. If the records have long-term value, the ability to convert them to a new system is extremely important. If the records are permanent, this ability is crucial. One alternative to converting the medium may be an indexing and retrieval system that is flexible enough to accommodate several media. In any case the ability to grow and change should be considered.

Resource Requirements

The medium used for records influences the costs of the system, where they occur, and how they appear in the budget. The costs of paper are generally diffused throughout the system. While the costs may be higher, they are much harder to quantify and focus on. Even when a change is positive, the resources to make the change may not be available.

- *Capital expenditures.* Probably the most important issue is to be sure that costs are fully identified. The initial equipment cost is often the tip of the iceberg. Maintenance, growth costs, and transition costs must be included. Most conversions take time. Very often both the old and new system must run simultaneously for some period of time. Be suspicious of a manufacturer or vendor who implies that change-over is instantaneous. Costs should be projected over the life of the project. Savings should also be projected carefully. Conversion and change-over costs will probably increase operating costs initially.

- *Personnel.* Often the costs for personnel savings are overestimated. For example, a system that goes from a central fileroom to a centralized optical disk will have to keep the central fileroom in operation until the files are phased out and/or converted. Initially, personnel costs may increase. If staffing level reductions are planned, the positions to be deleted should be identified. The remaining jobs often require more skills and a higher pay grade. Cost savings may be offset by severance costs, increased training needs, and higher paying positions. A highly automated system also requires support by people with a high level of skills.

- *Space.* Space requirements can be dramatically, but not completely reduced. At a minimum, space is needed to house equipment. Microfilm and optical image systems require room to prepare records. Change-over and conversion requirements may temporarily increase space costs. If space is to be released, a realistic timetable should be set.

- *Costs proportionate to value.* The cost of the system should reflect the importance of the records to the organization as a whole. Highly technical systems often require high operating budgets as well as increased management attention.

Solution Selected

The selection of a solution should be driven by what is best for the organization not what vendor or technology has the most features. The importance of the vendor varies in proportion to the investment and the unique qualities of the system. If the vendor is the only one available to support a complex system, then the relationship with the vendor is essential.

- *Alternatives considered.* The recommendation should show that a large number of alternatives have been considered. The consideration may be brief, but should indicate that those performing the evaluation were open to solutions to a problem rather than seeking to justify a purpose. Two to five vendors should be examined carefully and given serious consideration.

- *Based on organization's priorities and needs.* The needs and priorities of the organization should be set in advance. Features that are available and useful from different vendors can be added where they fit the needs of the organization. A weighted list of needs should serve as a yardstick to measure alternate solutions. Vendors should be measured against this yardstick rather than compared against each other. Comparisons should not be based solely on comparing features. All features are not equal and all are certainly not needed.

- *Is the entire solution needed?.* Sometimes 90% of the benefits accrue from 10% of the solution. Make sure each piece of the solution contributes in proportion to the resources it requires.

- *Vendor.* As a system increases in complexity, the vendor (or vendors) becomes a more essential component of success. Vendors should be scrutinized carefully to be sure they can deliver on their promises.

- *Proprietary equipment and software.* One problem with new technology is that fewer systems meet widely accepted standards. Many optical disk systems that utilize rewriteable or WORM technology incorporate proprietary software or hardware. If the company goes under or discontinues support of these products, records can be lost because they can no longer be accessed. Proprietary compression schemes, in particular, can cause problems in the future. They could prevent the transfer of records from one system to another. Some optical disk reading and writing schemes are also proprietary.

- *Acceptable experience base.* Someone has to be a vendor's first customer. Few vendors have sold large numbers of optical imaging systems. The choice of vendor for simple, standard systems is not critical. The combination of customer base, experienced personnel, and technical expertise for any vendor should be acceptable for the situation.

Potential Problem Areas

Very careful attention should be given to personnel requirements, indexing needs, migration paths, and conversions. These are potential trouble areas. Inadequate planning can mean the difference between success and failure.

- *Indexing.* Indexing records can be extremely time consuming. As the storage becomes more random, the importance of indexing increases.

  An activity that is both essential and time-consuming creates the potential for failure. Index only what is really needed when retrieving and managing the records. The impulse to over-index and cross-reference should be discourag. Every effort should be made to guarantee that information is keystroked only once. This usually means having the ability to share information between databases and even computer systems. Generally an experienced person can input 7,000 keystrokes per hour. If the staffing does not reflect this requirement or explain how higher input will be sustained, it is unlikely that estimated production levels can be met.

- *Conversions.* Changing records from one medium to another is very costly. It seems inevitable that it will cost more and take more time than projected. Conversions can not always be avoided. When they are undertaken, the costs must be carefully projected and the alternatives to full conversion carefully explored. Section 6 discusses the challenges presented by conversions.

- *Adequate time allowed for document preparation.* Microfilm and optical imaging systems usually involve filming or scanning paper records. The records must be prepared prior to capture. This usually involves from thirty to sixty percent of total conversion time. A careful assessment must be done of the amount of preparation. Preparation time is often underestimated and can create bottlenecks. Inadequate preparation will seriously detract from the quality of the finished project.

Media Selection

- *Life of medium matches record life.* A major difference among the media is the expected life of the records. The life of the medium includes both the life of the material and the equipment needed to view it. Paper requires no special equipment. Microfilm requires equipment, but it is standard and available. Magnetic and optical disk require both specialized equipment and software. The equipment may become obsolete before the medium deteriorates.

- *Strengths of medium matches needs.* Table 27 lists the strengths, weaknesses, and best applications for each medium. This table is a generalized synopsis. Particular applications may be designed to counteract weaknesses. However, this table does provide a basis for asking questions and investigating proposals.

A project with potential, but many questions, need not be rejected outright. One alternative is to keep the current medium and improve management. Another alternative is to phase in a system as budget constraints permit. The planning team can be asked to investigate further. More options can be considered. However at some point more investigation is not productive. When the impact of the change is extensive, a pilot project may be the only way to evaluate a system. If a change involves a conversion and a change in work habits, the chances of success can be endangered by the shear magnitude of the change. A pilot project can help provide better data for determining staffing needs for indexing and document preparation, allow for testing of procedures, point out unforeseen problems, and validate estimates of costs and savings.

This guide does not provide easy answers. It does provide a framework for you and your staff to analyze your records and organization, more information about alternatives, and an approach to match needs with a suitable technology. You provide the common sense and knowledge of your organization. May your decisions be wise.

<h1 style="text-align:center">Table 27: Comparative Strengths and Weaknesses of Media</h1>

Paper	Magnetic	Microfilm	Optical
Strong Areas			
– Versatile and flexible – Best ergonomic design-easy for people to use – Least equipment investment – With care, very long life expectancy – Most acceptable, legally	– Very fast access – Good standards – Excellent availability -everyone on system can have access to same information – Can be used with other media to manage work flow – Easily updated	– Saves storage space – Records retain integrity-no losses, misfiles, or missing pages – Low bulk – Inexpensive copies – Long life expectancy – Can speed retrieval – Most systems adhere very well to established standards – Equipment tends to ber interchangeable – Well-tested legal acceptability	– Saves space – Short turnaround time – Excellent control over documents and workflow – Records retain integrity – Can add and replace records – Can link computer database with record information – Very fast retrieval – Excellent availability -everyone on system has access to original – Can store both images and machine-readable records

Table 27: (Continued)
Comparative Strengths and Weaknesses of Media

Paper	Magnetic	Microfilm	Optical
Weak Areas			
– Hard to control – Easily lost – Damaged easily – One person at a time can have access to original – Labor intensive	– Special equipment needed – Very vulnerable to inadvertant change or loss – Not a permanent record – Must be substantiated by documentation	– Special equipment needed – Difficult to add a record or update it – Not as easy to use as paper – Must convert most documents – Conversion time can interrupt workflow – Limited use during processing	– Limited life expectancy – Special equipment needed – Restricted to cmpatible equipment and software throughout life of system – Easier to use than film, but not as easy as paper – Very high cost per user – High cost to add user – Legal acceptance has not been well tested; probably good with short term, but questionable for long-term documents – Records must be converted
Best Suited For			
– Small collections of records – Records with limited uses – Very short term records – Records with low value – Very long, multi-page records – Unitized records that are active over a very long period of time	– Well-suited to relational and draft records – Transitory information – Information designed to manage and locate other records – Very fast access to discrete information – Information that needs to be compiled in different ways for reporting – Body of information that needs to be shared easily	– Medium to high volume with low to medium retrieval rate – Medium to high value – Vital records – Copies of entire collections are needed – Storage of inactive records – Very long retention period – Stable information with few additions or deletions – Records where file integrity is important – Space savings are critical – Best suited to transactional, reference, or inactive, unitized records – Well-suited to some publication types	– Low to medium value with high value – Captured prior to processing – Controlling records during processing reduces errors and/or transaction period – High reference rate for short period – Life of records under five years – Fast access to documents needed – Information is suitable for publication – Work process is valuable to organization – Best suited to transactional records – CD-ROM can be good choice for publications and reference material – Can be good choice for storage of machine-readable data

Bibliography

1. "A Book of Verse, A Jug of Polymers". *Economist* 306 (February6,1988): 85.

2. "Adams, Russ. *Sourcebook of Automatic Identification and Data Collection.* New York: Van Nostrand Reinhold, 1990.

3. "An Optical Disk Primer (Part 1)". *Records and Retrieval Report.* October1987.

4. "An Optical Disk Primer (Part 2)". *Records and Retrieval Report.* November 1987.

5. Andrews, Harry. "Technological Advances and the Future of Electronic Imaging". *IMC Journal* 25 (September/October 1989):6+.

6. "Application Study: Canada's Investors Group and Document-Image Processing". *IMC Journal* 25 (March/April 1989):24+.

7. Arps, Mark. "CD-ROM Technology Hurt By Myths". *Computer Technology Review* 10 (September 1990): 30-36.

8. Aschner, Katherine. *Taking Control of Your Office Records.* White Plains, NY: Knowledge Industry Publications, Inc., 1983.

9. "Backup Strategies for Networks". *PC Today* 5 (January 1991): 37-41.

10. Balough, Ann. "The Media Decision: Factors in Choosing a Medium for Your System (Part 1)". *The Records and Retrieval Report* 5 (December 1989).

11. Balough, Ann. "The Media Decision: Factors in Choosing a Medium for Your System (Part 2)". *The Records and Retrieval Report* 6 (January 1990).

12. Balough, Ann. "The Media Decision: Factors in Choosing a Medium for Your System (Part 3)". *The Records and Retrieval Report* 6 (February 1990).

13. Barcomb, David. *Office Automation: A Survey of Tools and Technology.* Bedford, MS: Digital Equipment Corporation, 1981.

14. Barr, Robert D. "CAR Systems are on the Upswing". *IMC Journal* 25 (January/February 1989):5+.

15. Barr, Robert D. "Microfilm or Optical Disk: The Choice is Between Systems, Not Media". *IMC Journal* 24 (March/April 1988):7-8.

16. Beiswinger, George L. "Multipurpose Papers Fill Most Office Needs Today". *Office: Magazine of Information Systems and Management* 109 (May 1989): 78-80.

17. Black, David. "The New Breed of Mixed-Media Image Management Systems". *IMC Journal* 25: (January/February 1989): 9+.

18. Blechschmidt, J., H.-J. Naujock and D. Arnold "New Outlook for Utilization of Waste Paper in Paper Manufacture". *Prezglad Papier* 41 (February 1985): 44-48 (Poland).

19. Bogue, David T. "Nothing a Pseudonym Couldn't Fix". *INFORM* 5 (January 1991): 12-29.

20. Bookstein, Abraham and Shmuel T. Klein. "Compression, Information Theory, and Grammars: A Unified Approach". *ACM Transactions on Information Systems* 8 (January 1990): 27-49.

21. Bovee, Donna. "Document Conversion Methodology". *Optical Information Systems* (July-August 1990): 179-182.

22. Brathal, Dan. "Variety in Document Management: Format Follows Function". *IMC Journal.* Volume 24 (September/October 1988):19-21.

23. Brindza, Stephen. "Advancing Technology Homes in on Printing". *Modern Office Technology* 33:102-106.

24. Bubble Jet Printing for Reliability and Versatility". *Office Equipment and Products (Japan)* 16 (November 1987): 50-52.

25. "CALS Program Offers Technical Document Benefits". *Electronic Publishing and Printing* 5 (May 1990): 42-47.

26. Canning, Bonnie. "Critical Success Factors". *IMC Journal* 24 (September/October 1988) : 40.

27. "CAR in Records Management-1988". *Records and Retrieval Report.* September 1988.

28. Casurella, Joseph E. "CAR Versus Paper Files: Hard Facts About Software Driven Systems" *IMC Journal.* 24 (January/February 1988):14.

29. Cinnamon, Barry. "Optical Disk Applications". *IMC Journal* 24 (July/August 1988): 19-22.

30. Claydon, P. "Recycled Fiber - Major Furnish Component in Quality Newsprint Production". CPPA Technical Section Newsprint Conference, Montreal (September 26-28, 1989): 121-126.

31. Cole, Malcom. "Workplace Streamlined, Wood Reprieved". *Accountancy* 102 (October 1988): 84+.

32. Connell, John. "Image Processing: The Next Breakthrough" *IMC Journal* 22 (March/April 1986): 18+.

33. Date, C. J. *An Introduction to Database Systems: Volume 1.*Reading, Massachusetts: Addison -Wesley Publishing Company (1990).

34. Dauplaise, D. L. "A Balancing Act: Defining the Variables of Wet-End Chemistry". *PIMA Magazine* 67 (October 1985): 28-30.

35. Denley, M. Michael. "Optical Disk: Choosing the Right Size". *IMC Journal* 26 (November/December 1990): 16-17.

36. *Dictionary of Printing and Bookmaking.* Howard Lockwood and Company Publishers, 1967.

37. Ferelli, Mark. "Digital Paper Ideal for Data Compression". *Computer Technology Review* (August 1990): 25.

38. Fields, Howard. "House Unit Hears Testimony on Availability of Acid-Free Paper". *Publisher's Weekly* (May 26, 1989): 17.

39. Fisher, Marsha J. "Digital Paper Promises Cost, Storage Gains for Optical Media". *Datamation.* 34 (May 15, 1988): 32+.

40. Forester, W. K. "Recycling of Neutrally Sized Calcium Carbonate-Filled Paper". *TAPPI Conference* Hollywood, Florida (November 3-7, 1986): 141-145.

41. Frank, John W. "Micrographics And Optical Disk — Friend Or Foe". *IMC Journal* 24 (July/August 1988):-7-9.

42. "From Carbonless Paper to Photos". *Chemical Week* 135 (February 6, 1985): 44.

43. Giles, Peter. "Optical Disk Applications: Now That We Have Them — What are They Good For?". *IMC Journal* 23, 4 (1987): 22+.

44. Godwin, Jim. "Floptical Technology Marries Optical Disk and Magnetic Memory", *Computer Technology Review* 10 (Fall 1990): 65-70.

45. Gordon, Doug and Nigel Etherington. "What Do Optical Disk Service Bureaus Have to Offer". *Inform* 1 (May 1989): 21-29.

46. Graham, Gordon. "The World on a Disk". *Canadian Business* 63 (May 90). 75-72.

47. Grantham. Tim. "The Billion Byte Avalanche". *Canadian Data Systems* 22 (June 1990: 24-29.

48. Grigsby, Mason. "The Integration and Use of Write-Once Optical Information Systems". *IMC Journal* 23 (1987): 9+.

49. Grotophorst, Clyde W. "Keyless Entry: Building a Text Database Using OCR Technology". *Library Hi Tech* 7 (November 1989): 7-15.

50. Hall, Peter R. "Solid Ink Technology Solves Problems and Offers New Applications". *Computer Technology Review* 8 (Winter 1988): 105-109.

51. Hall, P. A. V. and S. Papadopoulos. "Hypertext Systems and Applications". *Information and Software Technology* 32 (September 1990): 477-490.

52. Hallen, Gary. "Document Retrieval for People Who Don't Care". *IMC Journal* 24 (September/October 1988): 9-12.

53. Harvey, David A. "State of the Media". *Byte* 15 (November 1990): 275-281.

54. "How Compression Works". *PCToday* 5 (January 1991): 55.

55. Hoy, John. "Only a True WORM is Worth Protecting". *Computer Technology Review* (November 1990): 22-24.

56. "Imaging White Paper: Results from the Imaging Work Group". *Optical Information Systems* (May/June 1990): 140-147.

57. "Imaging". *Records and Retrieval Report.* December 1989.

58. "Integrating Information Carriers". *Records and Retrieval Report.* March 1988.

59. Jenkins, Tom. "Good Records Management". *Office Systems '89* 6 (May 1989): 55-59.

60. Johnston, Ron. "Erasable Optical to Dominate All Storage?". *Computer Technology Review* 10 (October 1990): 22-23,42.

61. Jordahl, Gregory. "COLD Warms Up". *INFORM* 5 (January 1991): 15-18.

62. Kato, Hirokazu. "Plain Paper Facsimiles Span the Globe". *Office Equipment and Products (Japan)* 15 (March 1986): 59-60.

63. Kimura, Yoshiaki. "Inside the Ink-Jet Printer: Better Methods and Systems". *Office Equipment and Products (Japan)* 13 (June 1984): 38-41.

64. King, Dennis D. "Color Dot Matrix Print Quality Depends on Ink and Ribbon Technology". *Computer Technology Review* 6 (Winter 1985): 145-149.

65. Kondo, Yoshiaki. "As Printer and Typewriter Hardware Change, Ribbons are Being Improved to Keep Pace". *Office Equipment and Products (Japan)* 14 (July 1985): 41-42.

66. Kondo, Yoshiaki. "Direction of Development for Wire-Dot and Thermal Transfer Ribbons". *Office Equipment and Products (Japan)* 16 (May 1987): 56-57.

67. Larsen, Louis M. *Industrial Printing Inks*, Reinhold Publishing Corp., 1962.

68. Levy, Joel H. "Trend and Forecasts: OA and the Next Nine Months". *Administrative Management* 49 (April 1988): 17.

69. Lexington, Ann. "Micrographics and Total Information Management". *Office: Magazine of Information Systems and Management* 109 (February 1989)

70. Lion, Karina L. "DATs a Solution". *Byte* 15 (November 1990): 323-328.

71. Lundeen, Gerald W. "Preservation of Paper Based Materials: Present and Future Research and Developments in the Paper Industry". In *Conserving and Preserving Library Materials,* edited by Kathyrn Luther Henderson and William T. Henderson. University of Illinois, 1981. pp. 73-85.

72. Malor, Hugh. "Data Structures for CD ROM". *Bulletin of ASIS* 13 (August/September 1987): 18, 20.

73. Marley, M. E. "Secondary Fiber Improves the Quality of Newsprint". *Paper Technology* 30 (November 1989): 46-47.

74. McCormick, John A. *A Guide to Optical Storage Technology.* Homewood, Illinois: Dow-Jones Irwin, 1990.

75. McCready, Scott. "Optical Disk-Based Systems: Japanese and American Approaches". *IMC Journal* 25 (March/April 1989): 33+.

76. *McGraw Hill Encyclopedia of Science and Technology*, Volume 9, 1987, p. 171-176

77. Merchant, Alan B. *Optical Recording: A Technical Overview.* Reading, Massachusetts: Addison-Wesley, 1990.

78. Mims, Julian. "Optical Disk, Micrographics, and You". *IMC Journal* 26 (November/December 1990): 9-12.

79. Morgan, Ron. "Color Thermal Transfer Printers Provide Output on Plain Paper or Film". *Computer Technology Review* 6 (Winter 1985): 151-155.

80. Morrow, Carolyn Clark. *The Preservation Challenge.* Knowledge Industries Publications, 1983.

81. Nibler, R., A. Raedels, and M. Johnson. "Requirement Definitions of Data-Entry Productivity and Error Reporting System and Presentation of On-Site Experiment". *Information and Software Technology* 32 (September 1990): 470-476.

82. Nicke, R. and M. Tappe. "Paper Production in Neutral Medium". *Zellstoff Papier* 37 (January/February 1988): 16-18 (German).

83. "Optical Memory Systems". *Records and Retrieval Report.* February 1988.

84. "Paper for Computer Printers". *Records and Retrieval Report.* June 1989.

85. Parish, Tom. "Crystal Clear Storage". *Byte* 15 (November 1990): 283-288.

86. Parsaye, Kamran, Mark Chignele, Setrag Khoshafian, and Harry Wong. *Intelligent Databases: Object-Oriented, Deductive Hypermedia Technologies*. New York: John Wiley and Sons, 1989.

87. Passavanti, Bill. "Side by Side". *Byte* 15 (November 1990): 304-305.

88. Payne, Hunt. "Substrate Advances Critical to Small Drive Design". *Computer Technology Review* 10 (Fall 1990): 49-55.

89. Paznik, Megan Jill. "Optical Disk Storage Will Win But There are Problems". *Administrative Management* 49 (April 1988): 16.

90. Paznik, Megan Jill. "Optical Disk versus Micrographics". *Administrative Management* 49 (April 1988): 18+.

91. Plume, Terry. "Optical Disk Systems — Technology". *IMC Journal* 24 (January/February 1988): 29+.

92. Podio, Fernando L., Remigius Onyshczak, and Eduardo Sanchez Villagran. "Standardization of Testing Methods for Optical Disk Media Characteristics at NIST". *Optical Information Systems* (July/August 1990): 174-178.

93. Rancis, Art. "Helical Scan is Achieving High Densities". *Computer Technology Review* 10 (July 1990): 25-32.

94. "Records Management for the 1990's". *Records and Retrieval Report*. October 1988.

95. Reinhardt, Andrew. "Playing Catch-Up". *Byte* 15 (November 1990): 228-279.

96. "Relational Databases: A New Approach to Technical Illustration". *Electronic Publishing and Printing* 5 (May 1990): 20-28.

97. Ricks, Betty R. and Kay F. Gow. *Information Resource Management*. Cincinnati, OH: South-Western Publishing Co., 1984.

98. Robeck, Mary F., Gerald F. Brown, and Wilmer O. Maedke. *Information and Records Management*, Glencoe Publishing. 1974.

99. Roby, Christine. "Multifunction Technology Achieves Data Security". *Computer Technology Review* (November 1990): 22-24.

100. Rosenberg, Jim. "What Goes into Making No-Rub Inks". *Editor and Publisher* 122: 26+.

101. Ryan, Bob. "Entering a New Phase". *Byte* 15 (November 1990): 289-296.

102. Ryan, Bob. "The Once and Future King". *Byte* 15 (November 1990): 301-306.

103. Saffady, William. *The Automated Office: An Introduction to the Technology*, 1981, National Micrographics Association.

104. Saffady, William. *Optical Disks vs. Micrographics: As Document Storage and Retrieval Technologies*. Westport, Connecticut: Meckler Corp. 1988.

105. Sceli, W. Clair. "Micrographics and/or Optical Disk? Ideas to Help You Make the Right Decision". *IMC Journal* 23 (1987): 26+.

106. Schneider, J. "New Prospects for the Use of Starch in the Pulp Mass". *Industria Carta* 25 (January 1987): 37-39 (Italian)

107 Schowen, Jeffrey C. "Micrographic Economics". *Inform 1* (May 1989): 36+.

108. Seto, Tadoa. "Development of Ink-Ribbon Accelerating Marketability of Thermal Transfer Printers". *Office Equipment and Products (Japan)* Volume 14 (November 1985): 34-36.

109. Seto, Tadoa. "The Elements of Ink Ribbons Determine a Printer's Impact". *Office Equipment and Products (Japan)* 14 (May 1985): 74-75, 88.

110. Sharp, Kevin R. *Automatic Identification: Making It Pay*. New York: Van Nostrand Reinhold, 1990.

111. Shishikura, Yohichi. "A Brief Overview of Thermal Control Printer/Plotters". *Office Equipment and Products (Japan)* 16 (August 1987): 40-43.

112. Simpson, David. "Where Should You Use Rewritable Optical?". *Systems Integration* (May 1990): 62-74.

113. Siragusa, Gail. "Archival Records Storage - Microfilm vs. Paper". *Administrative Management* (December 1985): 56-57.

114. Skupsky, Donald S. (Editor). *Legal Requirements for Business Records: Guide to Records Retention and Recordkeeping Requirements.* Denver, Colorado, Information Requirements Clearing House. Updated Annually.

115. Smith, Milburn D. III. *Information and Records Management: A Decision-Maker's Guide to Systems Planning and Implementation.* New York: Greenwood Press, 1986.

116. Sorenson, D. "Environmental Concerns, Economics Drive Paper Recycling Technology". *Pulp Paper* 64 (March 1990): 56-57.

117. Spector, Stephen, ed. *Essays in Paper Analysis,* 1987. Associated University Press.

118. "Storing Paper". *Records and Retrieval Report.* September 1987.

119. Subt, Sylvia S. Y. "Xerographic Quality Control". *Inform* (July 1987): 10 +.

120. Sullivan, Roger K. "Image: The Next Information Frontier". *IMC Journal* 25 (May/June 1989): 24+.

121. Sullivan, Kristina B. "Signs Point to Corporate Growth of FDDI". *PC Week* 8: (January 7, 1991): 41-52.

122. Sweetman, D. "New Printing and Writing Grade of Papers Contains 100% Recycled Furnish". *Pulp Paper Canada* 91 (May 1990): 34.

123. Thatcher, Bruce. "Laser and LED Array Technologies in Non-Impact Printing". *Computer Technology Review* 9 (May 1989): 89-95.

124. *The Illustrated Science and Invention Encyclopedia.* Volumes 5, 11, and 13. H.S. Stuttman, 1983.

125. "Toners: The Technology Explosion That's Shaping A $1Billion Industry". *Chemical Week* 136 (January 30, 1985): 64+.

126. Ullman, Jeffrey D. *Principles of Database Systems.* Rockville, Maryland: Computer Science Press (1982).

127. Vaughan-Nichols, Steven J. "Getting Your Bytes Worth". *Byte* 15 (November 1990): 331-336.

128. Waegmann, C. Peter. *Handbook of Record and Space Management.* Westport, Connecticut: Quorum Books, 1983.

129. Walter, Gerry. "An Overview: Technology and Application Status of Optical Disk Systems". *IMC Journal* 24 (July/August 1988):10-13.

130. Webster, John. "Printers and Plotters: Users Stay Cool Amid a Whirl of Options". *ComputerWorld* 23 (May 29, 1989): 51-53, 57-62.

131. Willis, Mike. "Review of Nonimpact Print Technologies". *Data Processing (UK)* 27 (April 1985): 33-36.

132. Yoda, Masashi. "Special Papers and Media for Color Thermal Printers". *Office Equipment and Products (Japan)* 13 (November 1984): 32-35.